D1432480

Building Vocabulary Skills

by
Bonnie L. Walker, Ph. D.

American Guidance Service, Inc.
4201 Woodland Road
Circle Pines, MN 55014-1796
1-800-328-2560

Grammar and Composition Skills

Printed in the United States of America

ISBN 0–7854–0944–0 (Previously ISBN 0–88671–964–X)

Product Number 90840

A 0 9 8 7 6 5 4 5 3 2

Contents

What Is a Root Word?

➤ A *root word* is a word or part of a word to which different beginnings and endings can be added. Adding different beginnings or endings creates new words with different meanings. Many root words in English were originally words in other languages. A large proportion of English root words were taken from the Greek and Latin languages.

You can often figure out the meaning of a new word by finding the root word within it.

Example: What does *portable* mean?
The root word *port* means "to carry."
Portable refers to something that is "able to be easily carried."
I have a *portable* sewing machine.

We build words by adding *prefixes* (word beginnings) and *suffixes* (word endings) to root words. In the example above, the suffix *-able* was added to the root word *port* to form the word *portable.*

A Think of six other words with the root word *port*. Write them in the spaces below.

1. _____   4. _____

2. _____   5. _____

3. _____   6. _____

B Look at the list of words below. Circle the root word. Then match each word to its meaning. Use a dictionary, if necessary.

Cred is a Latin root word meaning "to believe."

1. _____ incredible   a. ready to believe

2. _____ discredit   b. believable

3. _____ credence   c. loss of belief

4. _____ credible   d. unbelievable

5. _____ credulous   e. belief

6. _____ creditor   f. worthy of belief

7. _____ credibility   g. someone to whom a debt is owed

8. _____ creditable   h. power of inspiring belief

Our Greek and Latin Roots

In its long history, the English language has grown and developed through borrowing from other languages. For example, large numbers of Latin and Greek words were adopted by English speakers in Britain in the 500s and 600s A.D. Today, more than half of the words in the English language are of Greek or Latin origin.

Greek root	Meaning	Latin root	Meaning
auto	self	cogn	know
hemi	half	dict	speak
micro	small	liber	free
phob	fear	ment	mind
phys	nature	multi	many
polis/polit	city	numer	number
photo	light	pop	people
scope	see	temp	time
tele	far	term	end

A Circle the root words in the words below. Write the definition on the line next to each word. Then use the word in a sentence.

1. liberate _____

Sentence: _____

2. hemisphere _____

Sentence: _____

3. temporary _____

Sentence: _____

4. cognizant _____

Sentence: _____

5. mental _____

Sentence: _____

B Write two English words that contain each Greek or Latin root.

1. polis/polit   _____   _____

2. tele   _____   _____

3. pop   _____   _____

4. term   _____   _____

5. multi   _____   _____

Joining Root Words and Suffixes

➤ A *suffix* is "an ending to a word." Add a suffix to a root word to make a completely new word.

The suffixes *-ant, -ent, -ar, -er,* and *-or* all mean "a person who _____."
Examples:

attend	+	*-ant*	=	attendant	a person who attends
study	+	*-ent*	=	student	a person who studies
beg	+	*-ar*	=	beggar	a person who begs
train	+	*-er*	=	trainer	a person who trains
act	+	*-or*	=	actor	a person who acts

The suffix *-ist* means "a person who practices or studies _____."
Examples:

type	+	*-ist*	=	typist	a person who types, or who practices typing

A Circle the suffixes in each word below. Match the words with their meanings.

1. _____ president   **a.** a person who operates something, such as a bus or machinery

2. _____ operator   **b.** a person who writes

3. _____ pianist   **c.** a person who presides over an organization

4. _____ servant   **d.** a person who practices the piano

5. _____ writer   **e.** a person who is in charge of funds (*bursa* means "purse")

6. _____ bursar   **f.** a person who serves

B Add the suffix to each root word below. Write the new word in the space. Then write the meaning of the new word.

1. dance + er _____

Meaning: _____

2. harp + ist _____

Meaning: _____

3. sail + or _____

Meaning: _____

4. command + ant _____

Meaning: _____

5. reside + ent _____

Meaning: _____

Changing Verb Forms

We use special suffixes to change verb forms. Look at the examples below.

➤ Add -s to a verb when the subject of a sentence is a third-person singular noun.
Example: The officers *eat* at that restaurant often.   (third-person plural subject)
             The officer *eats* a sandwich.   (third-person singular subject)

➤ When we speak now about an action that has been completed, we use the present perfect tense. We form the present perfect of many irregular verbs by adding -en.
Example: We *take* our dog for a walk.   (present)
             We have *taken* our dog for a walk.   (present perfect)

➤ When we speak of an action that is going on now, we use the present progressive tense. Change a verb from present tense to present progressive tense with -ing.
Example: Ken and Mike *walk* to school.   (present)
             Today they are *walking* to school.   (present progressive)

➤ Change a regular verb from present tense to past tense with -ed.
Example: The horses *jump* the fence.   (present)
             The horses *jumped* the fence yesterday.   (past)

A Change these verbs from present to past. Add the suffix -ed. Write the new words on the lines provided.

1. start _____   4. rain _____

2. talk _____   5. laugh _____

3. jump _____   6. walk _____

B Use suffixes to make three different forms of the verbs below. An asterisk (*) marks the irregular verbs.

Example: joke   jokes, joked, joking

1. love _____

2. fall* _____

3. beat* _____

4. turn _____

5. want _____

Spelling Rules Drop the final -e when adding a suffix that begins with a vowel: tak*e*, tak*ing*; glu*e*, glu*ing*.

Double the final consonant when adding a suffix that begins with a vowel to one-syllable words that end in a vowel and a consonant: st*op*, st*opped*; s*it*, s*itting*.

Singular and Plural Nouns

Change a noun from singular to plural by adding the suffix *-s* or *-es*.

➤ Make most nouns plural by adding *-s*.

Example: One boat   Two boats   One wall   Many walls

➤ Add *-es* to nouns that end in *-s, -sh, -ss, -ch,* or *-x*.

Example: One church   Several churches   A box   Those boxes
              One wish   Three wishes   My guess   Our guesses

A Add the correct suffix to make each word plural.

1. dollar _____
2. watch _____
3. bush _____
4. curtain _____
5. fox _____
6. match_____
7. book _____
8. wish _____

9. business _____
10. branch _____
11. tax_____
12. tree _____
13. window _____
14. ribbon _____
15. bunch _____
16. latch_____

B Drop the suffix and write the singular form of the word.

1. grasses _____
2. benches_____
3. chairs _____
4. mixes _____
5. tables _____
6. speeches _____
7. dinners _____
8. waxes_____

9. ways_____
10. boys _____
11. brushes_____
12. witches_____
13. marshes _____
14. sixes _____
15. houses _____
16. coaches _____

Spelling Rules ✓ Of course, there are many plural nouns that do not follow the usual rule. For example, child + *ren* = children. Perhaps you can think of others.

Changing Verbs to Nouns

Change a *verb* (an action word) to a *noun* (the name of something) by adding a suffix to a word.

Verb	Suffix	New Noun
construct (to build)	*-ion*	construction (building)
arrange (to put in order)	*-ment*	arrangement (something in order)

■ Change each verb to a noun by adding a suffix. Write the meaning of the new word. Then write a sentence using the new word. Use a dictionary to check your work.

1. direct + *ion* _____   *Direct* means "to tell how to do something."

Meaning of new word:_____

Sentence: _____

2. assess + *ment* _____   *Assess* means "to judge the importance or value of."

Meaning of new word:_____

Sentence: _____

3. complete + *ion* _____   *Complete* means "to end" or "to finish."

Meaning of new word:_____

Sentence: _____

4. improve + *ment* _____   *Improve* means "to make better."

Meaning of new word:_____

Sentence: _____

5. predict + *ion* _____   *Predict* means "to tell the future."

Meaning of new word:_____

Sentence: _____

Spelling Rules ✓

Check the dictionary for the correct spelling when you add *-ion* to a word.

transport + *a* + *tion* = transportation   (Add an *a* plus *tion*.)

Other examples: present*ation*, inform*ation*, indent*ation*, condemn*ation*, recommend*ation*

vacate + *ion* = vacation   (Drop the final *e*.)

Other examples: relat*e*, rela*tion*; complet*e*, comple*tion*; prec*ise*, preci*sion*; confus*e*, confu*sion*; promot*e*, promo*tion*

From Noun to Adjective

Some nouns can be changed to *adjectives* (words that describe nouns) by adding *-ful* or *-less.* The suffix *-ful* means "full of _____." The suffix *-less* means "without _____."

Examples: care + *ful* = careful
                     Careful means "full of care" or "cautious."

                     meaning + *less* = meaningless
                     Meaningless means "without meaning."

 Add *-ful* or *-less* to each noun to form an adjective. Write the meaning of the new word. Then use the new word in a sentence.

1. joy + *less* _____   *Joy* means "happiness."

Meaning of new word:_____

Sentence: _____

2. play + *ful* _____   *Play* means "fun or recreational activity."

Meaning of new word:_____

Sentence: _____

3. help + *ful* _____   *Help* means "assistance" or "aid."

Meaning of new word:_____

Sentence: _____

4. hope + *less* _____   *Hope* means "expectation of success."

Meaning of new word:_____

Sentence: _____

5. boast + *ful* _____   *Boast* means "the act of bragging."

Meaning of new word:_____

Sentence: _____

Spelling Rules

If a noun ends with a *consonant + y,* change the *y* to an *i* before adding *-ful* or *-less.*

Examples: beauty + *ful* = beaut*iful*   pity + *less* = pit*iless*
               plenty + *ful* = plent*iful*   penny + *less* = penn*iless*

From Adjective to Noun

Build your vocabulary. Change adjectives to nouns by adding *-ness* to a word.
The suffix *-ness* means "the state of being _____."

Adjective	+	Suffix	=	Noun	Meaning
kind	+	*ness*	=	kindness	the state or habit of being kind
thankful	+	*ness*	=	thankfulness	the state of being thankful

Change the adjectives to nouns by adding *-ness*. Write the meaning
of the new word. Then write this word in a sentence.

1. *Great* means "more than ordinary," "above average," or "most important."

great + *ness*_____

Meaning of new word:_____

Sentence: _____

2. *Thoughtful* means "marked by careful thinking."

thoughtful + *ness*_____

Meaning of new word:_____

Sentence: _____

3. *Sad* means "not happy" or "full of sorrow."

sad + *ness*_____

Meaning of new word:_____

Sentence: _____

4. *Dark* means "without light."

dark + *ness*_____

Meaning of new word:_____

Sentence: _____

5. *Fearful* means "full of fear."

fearful + *ness*_____

Meaning of new word:_____

Sentence: _____

From Adjective to Adverb

Many adverbs are formed by adding the suffix *-ly* to adjectives. An *adverb* is a word that tells how, when, or where an action took place, or how much is meant.

Adjective			Adverb	Tells	Sentence
recent	+	*ly*	recently	when	We saw the movie *recently*.
careful	+	*ly*	carefully	how	Jody *carefully* cut the paper.
most	+	*ly*	mostly	how much	The accident was *mostly* my fault.
distant	+	*ly*	distantly	where	The town was *distantly* visible.

 Change each adjective to an adverb by adding *-ly*. Use the new word in a sentence. Then write what the adverb tells about the action in the sentence.

1. soft + *ly* _____

Sentence: _____

Tells _____

2. local + *ly* _____

Sentence: _____

Tells _____

3. annual + *ly* _____

Sentence: _____

Tells _____

4. playful + *ly* _____

Sentence: _____

Tells _____

5. slight + *ly* _____

Sentence: _____

Tells _____

Spelling Rules

When a word ends with a *consonant + y,* change the *y* to an *i* before adding *-ly*.

Examples: pretty + *ly* = prett*ily*   noisy + *ly* = nois*ily*

Vocabulary Builder

Many words from science are formed by combining root words with the suffix -*ology*, meaning "the study of _____."

Root	Meaning	New Word	Meaning
bio	life or life-form	bio*logy*	study of life
entom	insect	entom*ology*	study of insects

Note: If a root word ends in -*o*, add -*logy* instead of -*ology*.

Add the suffix -*ology* to each of the root words below to form a new word. Then write the meaning of the new word. Use a dictionary to check the meanings.

1. *crimin* means "crime"   New word: _____

Meaning of new word:_____

2. *zoo* means "life"   New word: _____

Meaning of new word:_____

3. *psych* means "soul" or "mind"   New word: _____

Meaning of new word:_____

4. *geo* means "earth"   New word: _____

Meaning of new word:_____

5. *chron* means "time"   New word: _____

Meaning of new word:_____

6. *cardi* means "heart"   New word: _____

Meaning of new word:_____

7. *anthrop* means "human being"   New word: _____

Meaning of new word:_____

8. *cosm* means "universe"   New word: _____

Meaning of new word:_____

9. *toxico* means "poison"   New word: _____

Meaning of new word:_____

10. *eco* means "environment"   New word: _____

Meaning of new word:_____

Understanding Prefixes

➤ A *root word* is a word or part of a word to which different beginnings and endings can be added to form new words. You can often figure out the meaning of a new word by finding the root word within it.

➤ A *prefix is* a syllable joined to the beginning of a root word to form a new word with a different meaning.

Here are two important prefixes that will help you understand many new words.

➤ *Semi-* is a prefix from Latin meaning "half" or "twice in a given period."

➤ *Bi-* is a prefix from Latin meaning "two" or "twice."

Example: *Semi-* means "half."
             Annual means "yearly."
             Semiannual means "happening every half year or every six months."

■ Use your knowledge of the prefixes *semi-* and *bi-* to fill in the blanks in the sentences below.

1. A cycle is a wheel. A *bicycle* has _____ wheels. (How many?)

2. A *bimonthly* meeting occurs every _____ months. (How many?)

3. Jack visits New York on a *semiannual* basis, or _____ a year.

4. *Ped* is a root word meaning "foot." Because people have _____ feet, they are called *bipeds*.

5. One half of a circle is called a _____.

6. A *bicuspid* is a tooth with _____ points. (How many?)

7. *Centennial* means "100 years." A *bicentennial* event happens every _____ hundred years. (How many?)

8. *Bifocals* are glasses with _____ different lenses for different focuses. (How many?)

9. A *binary* number system has only _____ digits: 0 and 1.

10. The *Star* is a *semiweekly* newspaper; it comes out _____. (How often?)

11. A *bilingual* sign is written in _____ languages. (How many?)

The Prefixes *Post-* and *Ex-*

➤ A *prefix* is a "beginning to a word." The prefix *post-* means "after in time." It can be used to form new words.

Base Words and Roots	Meanings of Roots	New Words
script (Latin *scribere*)	writing	postscript
graduate (Latin *gradus*)	grade or level	postgraduate
pone (Latin *ponere*)	to put or place	postpone
war (Middle English *werre*)	fighting or strife	postwar

A Fill in the blank with the correct word listed above.

1. Ginny added a _____ to her letter.

2. In the _____ period, the damaged towns were rebuilt.

3. The pianist had to _____ the concert because she was ill.

4. In his _____ program, Michael studied business.

The prefix *ex-* means "from" or "out." This prefix can also be used to form new words.

Base Words	Meanings of Roots	New Words
hale (Latin *halare*)	to breathe	exhale
pel (Latin *pellere*)	to drive	expel
cavate (Latin *cavus*)	hollow	excavate
pand (Latin *pandere*)	to spread	expand

B Fill in the blank with the appropriate word listed above.

1. The board of directors voted to _____ a member who had not attended regularly.

2. They had to _____ an acre of land to build the hotel.

3. The hot air caused the balloon to _____.

4. "You can _____ now," the doctor said to the patient who was holding his breath.

Etymology is the history of a word in a language. Many English dictionaries give an etymology for each word that tells what language the word originally came from and when the word first appeared in English.

The Prefixes *Pre-*, *Sub-*, and *Re-*

Example: Pre- is a prefix meaning "before." *View* means "to see."
              Preview means "to see before."

A Here are some other words that have the prefix *pre-*. Match these
words with their meanings. Use a dictionary, if necessary.

1. _____ predate   **a.** to tell a future event before it happens

2. _____ predict   **b.** to occur before in time

3. _____ preempt   **c.** to take something or act before another person can do so; to
                                 replace a regularly scheduled program on television

4. _____ preface   **d.** to build sections in a factory before they are completely
                                 assembled at the final location

5. _____ prefabricate   **e.** an introductory part before the main body of a book

Example: Sub- is a prefix that means "under" or "beneath." *Terra* means
              "earth."
              Subterranean means "beneath the earth."

B Here are some words that have the prefix *sub-*. Match these words
with their meanings.

1. _____ subzero   **a.** an underground passage, usually for trains

2. _____ submarine   **b.** slower than the speed of sound waves in the air

3. _____ subdivide   **c.** below a temperature of 0°

4. _____ subway   **d.** undersea

5. _____ subsonic   **e.** to divide into smaller sections

Example: Re- is a prefix meaning "again." *Unite* means "to bring together."
              Reunite means "to bring together again."

C Here are some words that have the prefix *re-*. Match these words with
their meanings.

1. _____ readjust   **a.** to find out something again

2. _____ reelect   **b.** to appear or to be seen again

3. _____ rediscover   **c.** to adjust or to fix again

4. _____ reappear   **d.** to make something again after it has been torn down

5. _____ rebuild   **e.** to vote someone into office more than once

Backwards and Forwards

A *prefix* can be added to the beginning of a word to change its meaning.

➤ *un-*   —a prefix meaning "not" or "the opposite of"
unholy   not holy
unlearned   not educated
unlawful   not legal; not lawful; against the law

➤ *un-*   —a prefix meaning "back" or "an action in reverse"
undo   to untie or to open
untie   to unfasten; to free from restraint
unmake   to take apart; to undo

A Decide what the prefix *un-* means in each of the words below. Write the letter that goes with the correct meaning in the space provided.

   A *un-* means "not" or "the opposite of" the root word
   B *un-* means "reverse the action" of the root word

1. unsnap _____   4. unlikely _____   7. unhinge _____

2. unknown _____   5. unpaid _____   8. unload _____

3. unkind _____   6. unlock _____   9. unseat _____

➤ *re-*   —a prefix meaning "to do again" or "back."
redo   to do again or to do over
retie   to tie again
remake   to make something again

B Add the prefix *re-* to each word below. Write the meaning of the new word in the space. Use each new word in a sentence.

1. new   New word: _____

Meaning: _____

Sentence: _____

2. copy   New word: _____

Meaning: _____

Sentence: _____

3. draw   New word: _____

Meaning: _____

Sentence: _____

Opposites Attract

➤ We can use prefixes to create antonyms. An *antonym* is a word that means the opposite of another word.

anti-	a prefix meaning "against"
pro-	a prefix meaning "in favor of" or "supporting"
in-	a prefix meaning "not"
dis-	a prefix meaning "the reverse" or "the opposite"
non-	a prefix meaning "not"

A Answer each question below.

1. In the senate race, Jack is pro-Sandy Wilson. Is Jack for or against Mrs. Wilson?

   _____

2. Earl led the antismoking campaign in Boston. Is Earl in favor of or against smoking?

   _____

3. Abraham Lincoln was antislavery. Did he think slavery was a good idea or a bad idea?

   _____

4. Everyone says Mike is antisocial. Does Mike like to be around people or does

   he prefer to be alone? _____

5. Lana is pro-sports. Does she like sports or dislike them? _____

6. Ellen's work was incorrect. Was it right or wrong? _____

7. Mary agrees with Tom, but Sandy disagrees. Who thinks Tom is right? _____

8. Jeremy is a nonsmoker. Does Jeremy smoke cigarettes? _____

9. Wilson Brothers is a nonprofit company. Does this company make a profit?

   _____

B Use a prefix to write a word with the opposite meaning of each base word. Use a dictionary, if necessary.

Examples: happy   *un*happy   interested   *un*interested
             social   *anti*social   stop   *non*stop

1. able _____

2. appear _____

3. pack _____

4. believer _____

5. approve _____

6. pleasant _____

7. sane _____

8. correct _____

Vocabulary Builder

Build your vocabulary with words containing the Latin root *ject,* which means "to throw." In each sentence below, *ject* is combined with one of the following prefixes.

pro- means "forward" or "before"
inter- means "among" or "between"
in- means "in," "into," or "within"
re- means "again" or "back"

de- means "down"
e- or *ex-* means "out"
ob- means "against"
sub- means "under"

Study the meanings of the prefixes. Then choose the correct meaning for the underlined word in each sentence.

_____ 1. The rude fans were <u>ejected</u> from the basketball game.

   a. thrown out   **b.** welcomed   **c.** walked out

_____ 2. Try to <u>project</u> the company's growth during the next six months.

   a. build   **b.** plan for the future   **c.** increase

_____ 3. Jackie was very <u>dejected</u> after he lost his bicycle.

   a. happy   **b.** hungry   **c.** downhearted

_____ 4. Paula <u>rejected</u> her friend's suggestions.

   a. accepted   **b.** refused to listen to   **c.** admired

_____ 5. The nurse <u>injected</u> the vaccine into the patient's arm.

   a. forced in   **b.** rubbed   **c.** poured

_____ 6. I'm sorry, but I must <u>object</u> to your statement.

   a. agree with   **b.** go against   **c.** question

_____ 7. The rocket became a <u>projectile</u> when it was fired.

   a. a circling thing   **b.** a tall thing   **c.** a thing thrown forward

_____ 8. May I please <u>interject</u> a comment here?

   a. put or throw in   **b.** take out   **c.** give

_____ 9. The prisoners were <u>subjected</u> to harsh punishment.

   a. written about   **b.** had a tendency to   **c.** forced to endure

_____ 10. The <u>projector</u> made the images appear on the dark screen.

   a. machine that casts   **b.** television   **c.** camera
       light on a screen

Words Made from Words

Build your vocabulary by learning to break words into their parts. A *compound word* is a word that is made up of two or more smaller words.

Examples: blue + berry = *blueberry*   side + walk = *sidewalk*

Do not confuse compound words with root words that have prefixes and suffixes. Prefixes, suffixes, and most roots cannot stand alone as words in English. For example, the parts of the word *ejection* are the prefix *e-*, the root *ject*, and the suffix *-ion*. None of these parts is a real word in English.

A Circle only the compound words in the list below.

1. sandbox
2. preview
3. ending
4. toolshed

5. boxwood
6. airplane
7. wonderful
8. typewriter

9. promote
10. bookmark
11. subject
12. contentment

B Write the two words that make up each compound.

Example: bookworm   *book   worm*

1. barefoot_____
2. chalkboard _____
3. everyday _____
4. daytime_____
5. railroad _____

6. basketball_____
7. overboard _____
8. salesperson _____
9. workbook _____
10. blackberry _____

C Join the following words to make compound words.

Example: base + ball   *baseball*

1. sun + light_____
2. look + out _____
3. bed + room _____
4. over + night _____
5. any + time _____

6. out + doors _____
7. horse + back _____
8. up + stairs _____
9. some + body _____
10. hand + book _____

Figuring Out Meaning

Use the meanings of the words that make up a compound word to figure out the meaning of the compound word.

Example: sailboat = sail + boat   A sailboat is a boat that has a sail.

A Join each pair of words to form a compound word. Then, write the meaning of the new word. Check your definition in a dictionary.

Example: play + ground = playground   An outdoor playing area.

1. under + line _____

Meaning: _____

2. yard + stick _____

Meaning: _____

3. rail + road _____

Meaning: _____

4. fire + place _____

Meaning: _____

5. head + rest _____

Meaning: _____

B Form as many compound words as you can with the words from the following list. Write the new words on the lines below.

Word List

out	drive	light	foot	head	over	in
flow	time	body	paper	house	side	way
line	hold	stool	room	sand	every	some

1. _____   6. _____   11. _____

2. _____   7. _____   12. _____

3. _____   8. _____   13. _____

4. _____   9. _____   14. _____

5. _____   10. _____   15. _____

Recognizing and Using Compounds

You can often figure out the meaning of new words by knowing what their parts mean.

A Circle the compound word in each sentence. Then, write the meaning of that word on the line. Use a dictionary to check your definitions.

1. We can not swim in the ocean today because of the jellyfish.

_____

2. Corinne is watching the raindrops fall into the puddles.

_____

3. The firefighters pulled on their coats and boots as fast as they could.

_____

4. Suddenly Kathy heard footsteps on the porch.

_____

5. Mrs. Turner asked the students to get out their notebooks.

_____

B Write the meaning of each word that makes up the compound word. Then, write the meaning of the compound word. Use a dictionary to check your definitions.

1. cross_____   road_____

crossroad _____

2. book_____   store _____

*bookstore*_____

3. half _____   time_____

halftime _____

4. back_____   track _____

*backtrack*_____

5. flag _____   ship _____

flagship _____

Vocabulary Builder

The word *self* combines with other words to form many useful compound words.

Self + a Root Word	
self-addressed	addressed to yourself (a self-addressed envelope)
self-taught	educated by your own efforts, without formal schooling
self-control	in command of your feelings and emotions
self-conscious	aware of your actions, feelings, etc.
self-defense	an action taken to protect yourself
self-explanatory	something that explains itself; needing no explanation
self-made	successful through your own efforts
self-pity	having pity for yourself; feeling sorry for yourself
self-satisfied	feeling pleased with your actions or accomplishments
self-service	the practice of serving yourself, as in a self-service store
self-sufficient	able to get along without help; independent
self-winding	capable of winding or turning itself, like a watch

A Replace each phrase in italics with one of the words above. The first one is done for you.

Randy Cooperman learned history by reading books at the library. He is

self-educated

~~*a person who educated himself.*~~ Also, Randy is *a person who became successful*

through his own efforts. He earned his fortune by being a top salesperson for a

company that sold watches *that could wind themselves* in stores *where people*

served themselves.

Randy learned *how to defend himself* at the local karate school. "I'd like to

be able to *take care of myself,*" Randy said.

"I have no *feelings of pity for myself,*" said Randy. "I have *control of myself.*

I am a person who is *satisfied with himself!*"

B Match the words below with their meanings.

1. _____ self-starter   **a.** becoming aware or discovering by yourself

2. _____ self-taught   **b.** good thoughts about yourself

3. _____ self-discovery   **c.** learned by yourself; self-educated

4. _____ self-respect   **d.** improving yourself by your own efforts

5. _____ self-help   **e.** a person who gets going without any help

Review Units 1–3

A Study the list of words below. Decide whether each word is a compound word or a root word with a prefix or suffix. Then write the word under the correct heading.

multiplex	handshake	diction	weekly	outcome	microcosm
armchair	phonology	meekness	distrust	clipboard	galloped
protest	teacup	horseplay	evergreen	springtime	violinist

Compound Words		Root Words + Prefixes or Suffixes	

B Read the sentences below. Use your knowledge of prefixes, suffixes, and root words to figure out what each underlined word means.

_____ 1. The film used in cameras is underlined{photosensitive}.

   a. sensitive to heat   **b.** sensitive to light   **c.** sensitive to pressure

_____ 2. After the snowstorm, the town was almost underlined{unrecognizable}.

   a. familiar   **b.** destroyed   **c.** impossible to know or recall

_____ 3. The guide could not answer all of our underlined{innumerable} questions about the space shuttle.

   a. too many to number   **b.** few   **c.** countable

_____ 4. The news reporter interrupted the underlined{telecast} of the president's speech.

   a. radio broadcast   **b.** television transmission   **c.** telegram

_____ 5. The great scientist wrote about her achievements in her underlined{autobiography}.

   a. story of someone's own life   **b.** best-known book   **c.** story of someone's life

_____ 6. Anita underlined{distrusted} the woman who had taken the money.

   a. believed   **b.** hated   **c.** did not have faith in

_____ 7. The man with the underlined{cosmopolitan} appearance said he had traveled around the world.

   a. ordinary   **b.** worldly   **c.** small-town

_____ 8. We needed underlined{semisweet} chocolate to make the cake.

   a. bitter   **b.** very sweet   **c.** slightly sweet

Parts of an Hour

Time is measured by parts of an hour. We can express the same time in words or numbers.

It is a quarter of twelve.

11:45

It is a quarter after twelve.

12:15

It is half past six.

6:30

■ Look at each clock. Write the time in words.

1. 9:30

1._____

_____

_____

2. 11:15

11:15

2._____

_____

_____

3. 7:30

3._____

_____

_____

4. 1:45

1:45

4._____

_____

_____

Expressing Time

Read the following sentences. Draw the hands on the clocks to show the correct time.

1. Bob has a dentist's appointment at 2:15 (a quarter past two).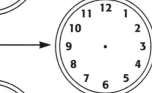

2. Lisa had to meet the car insurance salesperson at 8:30 (half past eight).

3. The party started at 9:30 (half past nine).

4. The bus is supposed to be at this stop at 6:45 (a quarter of seven).

5. Joan said the movie started at 10:15 (a quarter past ten).

6. Bill has to be at work at 6:30 (half past six).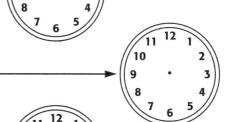

7. That clock is wrong—it says it is 4:15 (a quarter after four).

8. Actually, it is only 3:45 (a quarter of four).

9. Joe's job interview is at 7:45 (a quarter of eight).

10. Mark said he would pick us up at 10:30 (half past 10).

Time in Minutes

Lesson 3

Parts of an hour are also written in terms of minutes.

Examples:

2:20
It is twenty minutes after two
or two twenty.

2:55
It is five minutes before three
or two fifty-five.

A Write the following times in word form. Write each one two different ways. The first one has been done for you.

1. 9:45 *nine forty-five; a quarter of ten* _____

2. 8:15 _____

3. 6:30 _____

4. 3:55 _____

5. 4:10 _____

B Read the following sentences. Draw the hands to show the time on each clock.

1. Sue's appointment is at 8:20 (twenty minutes after eight). ➤

2. The party will start at 9:35 (twenty-five minutes before ten). ➤

3. School starts at exactly 8:10 (ten minutes after eight). ➤

4. The Smith family eats dinner every night at 6:05 (five minutes after six). ➤

5. The train will arrive at 11:40 (twenty minutes before twelve). ➤

Tomorrow and Tomorrow and Tomorrow

Time is also measured in days, weeks, months, and years. A *day* represents the amount of time it takes the earth to make one complete turn on its axis. A *year* is the amount of time it takes for the earth to circle the sun. A *month* is roughly the length of time it takes for the moon to complete its orbit around the earth. The length of a *week* is not scientifically defined. The seven-day week was used in ancient times by the Babylonians, Egyptians, and Hebrews.

➤ There are 31 days in the months of January, March, May, July, August, October, and December.
➤ There are 30 days in the months of April, June, September, and November.
➤ There are 28 days in February, except in a leap year, when February has 29 days. (Leap years occur every four years, except in century years—1900, for example. A leap year will not occur in a century year unless its number can be divided evenly by 400.)
➤ There are 52 weeks in a year.
➤ There are 12 months in a year.
➤ There are 7 days in a week.

■ Fill in each blank with the correct answer.

1. Jane's car payment is due on _____.(the last day in March)

2. I made a dentist's appointment for _____.(the last day in September)

3. Our grandfather was born on the 29th, the last day of _____ in a leap year.

4. There are _____ months in two years.

5. Megan's birthday is on _____.(the last day in November)

6. George Washington was born on _____.(the 22nd day of the second month)

7. There are approximately _____ weeks in every month.

8. Mary's party will be on _____.(the last day of April)

9. The mortgage payment is due on _____.(the first day of the year)

10. Patty's boss pays her every two weeks or _____ times a year.

11. The months of September, _____, _____, and November have 30 days.

12. The months of _____, March, _____, July, August, October, and December have 31 days.

13. Jerry has 60 months or _____ years to pay back his loan.

14. A leap year will occur in a _____ only if its number is divisible by 400.

Time Lines

In many countries, years are counted from the date of Christ's birth. If an event occurred before the birth of Christ, the year is followed by *B.C.* (before Christ). If an event occurred after the birth of Christ, the year is preceded by *A.D.* This abbreviation comes from the Latin words *anno Domini,* meaning "in the year of the Lord."

Example: The American Revolutionary War began in A.D. 1775.

A Use the time line below to answer the following questions. Write *B.C.* after or *A.D.* before each year.

2600	509	27	0	1350	1914	1969
pyramid of Khufu completed	Roman Republic established	Roman Empire began	birth of Christ	Renaissance began	World War I began	first landing on the moon

1. The Renaissance began in about _____.

2. In _____, the first humans landed on the moon.

3. The Egyptians built the pyramid of Khufu in about _____.

4. Which came first, the Renaissance or the Roman Empire? _____

5. Did World War I occur in the 1900s B.C. or the 1900s A.D.? _____

6. Which came first, the Roman Empire or the Roman Republic? _____

7. Did the Roman Empire begin in 27 B.C. or A.D. 27? _____

B Draw a time line based on your life. Start with the year you were born. Mark important events.

Suggestions: Mark your first year in school, dates of family events, accomplishments, etc.

Words about Time

The following words are used to express units of time or to describe how often something happens.

daily	every day		**midday**	noon
weekly	every week		**semimonthly**	twice a month
monthly	every month		**semiannual**	twice a year
yearly	every year		**decade**	10 years
annually	every year		**century**	100 years
biannual	every two years		**millennium**	1,000 years
twilight	just before dark		**eon**	indefinitely long period
dawn	the beginning of day		**moment**	very short period

Fill in the blanks with the correct words from the list.

1. Aunt Millie is 100 years old. She has lived through a _____.

2. This play was written a _____ ago. (1,000 years)

3. I have not seen Sue in an _____. (a very long time)

4. The year 1901 was the first year in this _____.

5. We waited a _____ for the light to change before driving on.

6. "Brush your teeth twice _____," said the dentist. (every day)

7. The board of directors meets _____. (once a year)

8. Jerome's family has _____ reunions, so he gets to see his cousins every two years.

9. The break of day is also called _____.

10. The time between 1980 and 1990 represents a _____.

11. If Carl jogs daily, he exercises _____ times in one week.

12. How many years are in two decades? _____

13. After the sun set, the children chased fireflies in the _____.

14. At _____, the sun is at or near its highest point.

It's Been a Long, Long Time!
I haven't seen you *in a dog's age.*
My goodness, it's been a *month of Sundays* since we got together.
It seems *like forever* since we saw each other.

U N I T 4

Around the world, people use *standard time zones* to measure time. The boundaries of the time zones are set according to the lines of longitude, which are used to divide the earth into equal sections from north to south.

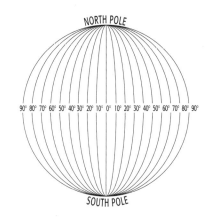

Lines of Longitude

| Pacific Time 9:00 A.M. | Mountain Time 10:00 A.M. | Central Time 11:00 A.M. | Eastern Time 12:00 noon |

Time Zones

In the United States (not including Alaska or Hawaii), there are four time zones. There is a one-hour difference in time between each zone.

Eastern Standard Time (EST)	Time in the states along the Atlantic Coast.
Central Standard Time (CST)	Time in the midsection of the United States.
Mountain Standard Time (MST)	Time in the Rocky Mountain region.
Pacific Standard Time (PST)	Time in the states along the Pacific Coast.

In the spring, we set our clocks ahead one hour ("spring forward"). That way, we get an extra hour of daylight. We call this time "Daylight Savings Time." In the fall, we turn our clocks one hour back again ("fall back"). Everyone gets an extra hour of sleep for one night!

 Fill in each blank with the correct answer.

1. The Super Bowl started at 6 P.M. in New York City. At what time did it actually begin in San Diego, California? _____

2. When do we get an extra hour of sleep: spring or fall? _____

3. John left Cleveland at 4 P.M. EST for Des Moines. The trip took two hours. Des Moines has Central Time. What time should he set his watch when he arrives? _____

4. It was eleven o'clock when James went to bed on the evening before Daylight Savings Time began. He changed his clock so that it would be correct in the morning. Did James change the time to (A) 10 P.M. or (B) midnight? _____

5. It's noon in Eugene, Oregon. What time is it in Miami, Florida? _____

Vocabulary Builder

There are many expressions based on time. Here are a few of them.

time killer	something we do to waste time
time-out	a break from an event
lose time	to get behind schedule
make time	to get ahead of schedule; to hurry so that you have extra time to do something else
waste time	to use time badly; to use it up needlessly
make up time	to catch up; to do something faster than you had planned; to get back on schedule
race against time	to try to complete an event before the time allowed is up
time is up!	you are out of time
good timing	doing something at the right moment in time
bad timing	doing something at the wrong moment in time
timed event	an event which is limited to a certain amount of time
killing the clock	trying to use up extra time in a timed event
run out of time	to use up all available time
spend time	to pass or take up time

Fill in the blanks with a word or phrase from the list above that completes the sentence. *Important:* There may be more than one correct response.

1. The pilot increased his speed to _____ he had lost due to a late departure from the airport.

2. A comedian must have _____ with jokes to be successful.

3. Laughing at the boss's joke at the wrong place was _____.

4. The quarterback called for a _____ on the field.

5. We _____ on the way home because of the heavy traffic.

6. Basketball and football games are examples of _____.

7. The basketball team tried to _____. They dribbled and passed the ball to keep the other team from scoring in the last minute of the game.

8. The men rushed to get their work done before the end of the day. It was a

_____.

9. "Television is a _____," says my Uncle Mike.

10. "Don't _____ when there is work to do," said the manager.

11. Work the test problems quickly, so you do not _____.

12. Jane likes to _____ reading books or playing sports.

Different Kinds of Language

People talk and express themselves in various ways. They use different words depending on the situation and on the area of the country in which they live.

formal, standard   language spoken exactly according to the rules of grammar
"Hello. How may I assist you?"

colloquial   conversational language; everyday language
"Hi. Need help with anything?"

dialect   language spoken in a certain region; dialects differ in terms of vocabulary, grammar, and pronunciation
"Sit down and have a cup o' char. The queen mum's on the telly."

jargon   technical language associated with a certain activity or group
"I just bought a PC with 32 megabytes of RAM."

slang   very informal language, often associated with a particular group
"Hey! What's the 411 on the new wheels?"

Read each statement. Identify the type of language.

A. formal   **B.** colloquial   **C.** dialect   **D.** jargon   **E.** slang

_____   1. "Good evening, gentlemen. How many will be dining with us tonight?"

_____   2. "I can carry y'all back to town in my car."

_____   3. "Wow, did you see that car? Now that's really *bad!*"

_____   4. "There are a lot of bugs in that software; maybe the upgrade is better."

_____   5. "Good-bye, everybody. Nice meeting you."

_____   6. "Let's ready up the place before Grandma comes home."

_____   7. "Two EKGs are needed in the ER."

_____   8. "Did you drink a pop or milk with your lunch?"

_____   9. "Mr. Brookman, may I present my aunt, Mrs. Sarah Carter."

_____   10. "We'll modem the data, which you can download."

_____   11. "Jerry, meet my best friend, Josh."

_____   12. "I didn't have enough moola to get in to see the flick."

The Way We Talk

Many words are used to describe the ways in which people talk.

chatter   to talk quickly and without stopping, usually about unimportant subjects
During the trip, the children *chattered* happily in the back seat of the car.

gibberish   meaningless speech or writing
"Don't talk *gibberish*," said Joe.

small talk   light, friendly conversation about common, everyday things
At lunch time, the workers engaged in *small talk* to relax.

discuss   to talk over; to consider both sides of an issue
Dewayne and Catherine were *discussing* a problem.

silent   quiet; not speaking
Sarah was *silent* all during dinner.

long-winded   talking at great length (often tiresome length) about a subject
Everyone thought that the speaker was *long-winded.*

wordy   using too many words to express an idea
"Don't be so *wordy*," said the newspaper editor. "We do not have much space for that story."

talkative   liking to talk; fond of talking
Toni is a very *talkative* person.

■ Fill in the blank with a word that best completes the sentence.

1. The professor said that the paragraph was too long. "Your writing is often very _____," she said.

2. The speech by the _____ mayor lasted three hours.

3. At lunch, the girls _____ about their summer vacations.

4. Rob is a very quiet person. Sam is the opposite. He is very _____.

5. Raoul talked so fast that no one could understand him. "That was _____ to me," said his friend Carlos.

6. The nickname "_____ Cal" was given to the 30th American president. Calvin Coolidge did not like to talk.

7. Donna and Si-ju met to _____ plans for their company's newsletter.

8. At dinner, the family engaged in _____ while they ate. No serious discussions were allowed.

The Way We Are

Here are some interesting words that we use to describe people.

mournful	very sad; sorrowful
ridiculous	very silly or absurd; causing laughter
well-bred	polite or genteel
bold	fearless
ravenous	very hungry or greedy in eating; also, very eager
adorable	very beautiful, lovely, or sweet

Answer each of the following questions.

1. Describe a situation that would make you mournful.

2. Tell about a time when you felt ridiculous.

3. Tell about an event when you were bold.

4. Who is the most well-bred person you know? Explain what it is about that person that gives you that opinion.

5. Describe a time when you were ravenous. Use as many details as possible.

6. Describe the most adorable person or animal that you know. Tell what they look like and how they act. Explain what they do that you find attractive.

It's High Time!

The word *high* comes from Old English. It has several meanings, including
➤ lofty
➤ in the air
➤ extending upward
➤ above others in rank or position
➤ a superior level or place

We combine *high* with many other words to produce words and phrases that we use.

high time	a very good time
high life	luxurious, expensive lifestyle
high-spirited	very happy
high and low	everywhere
high-minded	having high ideals or principles
high-rise	a building with many stories or floors
high-hat	(slang) snobbish
high-pressure	very persuasive, pushy
high-strung	highly sensitive or nervous
high sign	a secret warning signal
highborn	of noble birth

Fill in each blank with one of the expressions above.

1. Prince Charles of England is a _____ person.

2. We lived on the fortieth floor of the _____.

3. The car salesperson gave us a _____ sales pitch.

4. "Don't be snobbish or _____ with me, John," said Cassie.

5. "Give me the _____ if you see someone coming," said Julie as all the guests waited at the surprise party.

6. We had a _____ at the graduation party.

7. Suzy is known for being a cheerful, _____ person.

8. The carefree millionaire was known for pursuing the _____.

9. We searched _____ for our missing kitten.

10. The well-respected judge was considered to be a _____ woman.

Similes

A *simile* is a figure of speech that compares two things. The first word in a simile is often *like* or *as*.

 Similes can help us express our ideas. Write each expression in a sentence.

Example: Her *hands* were *as cold as ice* after she finished making the ice cream.
(The sentence compares the coolness of someone's hands to ice.)

1. as warm as toast

_____

2. as sweet as pie

_____

3. like roses

_____

4. as tall as an oak

_____

5. as pretty as a picture

_____

6. as light as a feather

_____

7. as proud as a peacock

_____

8. like sunshine

_____

9. as dry as a bone

_____

10. as quick as a wink

_____

Words That Sell and What They Mean

Certain words give us good feelings when we see or hear them. Some words give us bad feelings. Advertisers trying to sell us something use words to make us want to buy their products. Below is a list of words commonly used in advertisements by supermarkets or food producers to attract customers.

all-natural ingredients	ingredients that have not been changed through the use of chemicals or mechanical processing
artificial	made by humans
fresh	newly made; just picked; not cooked or frozen
healthy	promoting good health; feeling strong or good
fat-free	containing no fat
calorie	unit used to measure the amount of energy the body gets from food
low-calorie	describes foods containing a low number of calories
high-fiber	describes foods that contain large amounts of *fiber*, a material that helps the digestive organs work properly
diet	the kinds of foods that you eat regularly
balanced diet	a diet that provides all of the *nutrients* (vitamins, minerals, protein, etc.) your body needs

Write a definition for each item below.

1. low-calorie soft drink

   _____

2. artificial sweetener

   _____

3. fresh orange juice

   _____

4. high-fiber breakfast cereal

   _____

5. healthy appetite

   _____

6. fat-free snacks

   _____

7. poor diet

   _____

8. all-natural ice cream

   _____

Borrowed Words

Many words in the English language have been borrowed from other languages from around the world. You can find out which language a word originally came from by looking up the etymology of the word in a dictionary. An *etymology* is the history of a word. Etymologies in dictionaries may include the date when the word first appeared in English, the language the word came from, and changes in the word over time.

Original Language	Borrowed Words in English
African languages	chimpanzee (Bantu), mumbo jumbo (Mandingo)
American Indian languages	chocolate (Nahuatl), hurricane (Taino), moccasin (Algonquian)
Arabic	algebra, check, tariff
French	beef, danger, faith
German	flak, kindergarten
Hindi	jungle, pajamas, shampoo
Italian	balcony, carnival, cash
Japanese	kimono, tsunami, tycoon
Russian	bolshevik, czar
Spanish	alligator, cargo, mosquito

Match each word with its definition. The language or language group each word came from is identified in parentheses. Use a dictionary if you need help.

_____ 1. cargo   **a.** a tax on imported goods (Arabic)

_____ 2. chimpanzee   **b.** belief; trust; loyalty (French)

_____ 3. kimono   **c.** a long robe with wide sleeves (Japanese)

_____ 4. faith   **d.** a platform with a railing attached to the side of a building (Italian)

_____ 5. chocolate   **e.** title of the ruler of Russia before the revolution in 1917 (Russian)

_____ 6. tsunami   **f.** freight (Spanish)

_____ 7. czar   **g.** food prepared from roasted cacao beans (American Indian)

_____ 8. jungle   **h.** an African ape that lives in regions near the equator (African)

_____ 9. balcony   **i.** very thick forest (Hindi)

_____ 10. tariff   **j.** huge sea wave caused by volcanic activity or earthquake (Japanese)

Vocabulary Builder

Color terms can have important uses besides naming actual colors. The meaning of a color term may change, depending on the phrase or expression in which it is used. Consider the word *blue*, for example.

Expression	Part of Speech	Meaning
blue	adjective	sad; depressed
blue blood	noun	someone from a royal or socially important family; an aristocrat
blue-collar	adjective	related to workers who must wear work clothes or protective clothing on the job
out of the blue	adverb	unexpectedly; coming suddenly out of the unknown
true-blue	adjective	loyal
blue law	noun	a law that restricts certain activities on Sunday
bluenose	noun	someone with high moral principles
bluestocking	noun	an intellectual or literary woman. The word comes from the name given to a club in London in the 1700s that was made up mostly of women.
blue-pencil	verb	to edit or correct, as with a blue pencil

Fill in the blank with the expression that completes the sentence.

1. The editor _____ the reporter's story.

2. A woman who likes to read and study might be called a _____.

3. Tony got a letter from his cousin completely _____.

4. Because of the _____, the store was not open on Sunday.

5. The mayor's speech at the factory helped her win the _____ vote.

6. Everyone said that Howard's best friend was _____.

7. When their puppy was sick, the children were very _____.

8. The duke, the duchess, and other _____ attended the ceremony.

9. Cal was so strict about following the rules, he was called a _____.

Parts of Speech to Know

Noun	a word that is the name of a person, place, thing, or idea
Adjective	a word that describes a person, place, thing, or idea
Verb	a word that expresses an action or state of being

FOR YOUR INFORMATION

I'm just trying to make a living. **This is my livelihood.** **I just want a living wage.**

Making a living, livelihood, a living wage—these are ways that we describe our jobs and the money we earn. Getting a job is not enough. To get satisfaction and advancement in our work, we need to plan our careers. Writing a résumé is an important step in that plan.

A *résumé* is a summary of our work and educational experience. There are four main sections of a résumé:

➤ Personal information   ➤ Work experience
➤ Education   ➤ References

■ Start by getting your personal information together. Use the example below as your guide.

	Example	**Your Information**
Full name:	Joan Elaine Hartmann	_____
Street Address:	3091 Ocean Parkway	_____
City, State, ZIP code:	Berlin, MD 21811	_____
Telephone:	(301) 555-2123	_____
Date of Birth:	12/9/66	_____
Social Security Number:	214-32-3420	_____

Writing Your Résumé

Read the sample résumé below carefully.

Joan Elaine Hartmann
3091 Ocean Parkway
Berlin, MD 21811
(301) 555-2123

EDUCATION

1985-1986	Drafting and Surveying (12 credits), Berlin Community College.
1984	Graduate, Central High School.

POSITIONS

1987 to present	Drafter, Gerbers & Wilson, Architects, Berlin, MD.
1984-1987	Assistant graphics designer, Merton and Thomas, Graphic Specialists, Berlin, MD.

SUMMARY OF EXPERIENCE

Experience with Gerbers & Wilson includes drafting on several types of residential property including single-family homes, apartment buildings, and townhouses. Before joining Gerbers & Wilson, worked for three years as a graphics artist; also designed brochures, flyers, and announcements for many businesses.

REFERENCES

Jack Merton, Partner, Graphic Specialists, Berlin, MD.
Paula Splaine, Supervisor, Drafting Department, Gerbers & Wilson, Berlin, MD.

■ Write your résumé on your own paper. Include all necessary information. Follow the sample format above.

➤ Write your rough draft first.

➤ Check all information for accuracy.

➤ Write your final draft.

➤ Have your final résumé printed on a piece of $8\frac{1}{2}$-by-11-inch paper.

➤ Make copies of your résumé.

➤ Take copies of your résumé with you whenever you apply for a job.

Job Applications

A *job application* is a form we fill out when we ask for a job. Job applications help employers find out about your background and abilities. You can use information from your résumé to help you fill out a job application.

Here are some words used on job applications.

applicant	someone who is seeking a job
available	ready to begin working
immediate supervisor	your boss; the person to whom you report
not applicable (N/A)	the question does not apply to you
position title	the name of your job
reference	a person who will recommend you to someone else
skill	something you do well; an ability
transcript	an official educational history; usually a list of courses taken, including dates, number of credits, and grades. You can order transcripts from your school or college.

■ Match each term with its meaning.

1. _____ transcript
2. _____ position titles
3. _____ people who make good references
4. _____ immediate supervisor
5. _____ former
6. _____ applicant
7. _____ job skills
8. _____ not applicable

a. a person seeking a job

b. bookkeeping, filing, operating a computer

c. sales representative, cashier, manager

d. former teachers, supervisors, a minister

e. something from the past

f. something that does not apply to you

g. your boss

h. list of courses, dates, and grades

Completing a Job Application

Fill out a job application neatly, completely, and correctly. Your chances of getting a job will be greater if your writing is clear and easy to read.

■ Here is part of a job application. Fill in the information.

Today's Date _____

Applicant's Full Name _____
                         First   Middle   Last

Street Address _____
         Number   Street   Apt. No.   City   State   ZIP code

Social Security Number _____

Position Applied For _____

Date Available _____

Job Skills (List all) _____

Highest Year of School
Completed (Circle)   9   10   11   12   College 1   2   3   4   4+
                       Diploma Earned _____   Degree Earned _____

List current and previous positions. Start with your current position and work backwards.

Title	Company	Address	Dates Worked
Title	Company	Address	Dates Worked
Title	Company	Address	Dates Worked

List up to three references.

Name	Address	Phone	Type of Business
Name	Address	Phone	Type of Business
Name	Address	Phone	Type of Business

Words on a Paycheck

```
7-98
3212

MERCANTILE SAFE DEPOSIT                    CHECK DATE              CHECK NO.
AND TRUST CO.
BERLIN, MARYLAND                           1/23/96                90877

        Gerbers & Wilson, Architects
        12000 Prospect Square
        Berlin, MD 21811
                                                         AMOUNT OF CHECK
Three Hundred Eighteen and 24/100                        ***318.24

                                                         PAYROLL CHECK

PAY         HARTMANN, JOAN E.
TO THE      3091 OCEAN PARKWAY
ORDER OF    BERLIN, MD 21811

                                            Jack Gerbers
.ıl2   8242   256   ꞉689000250꞉          Authorized Signature
                                            Void after 90 days from check date
```

Study the paycheck above. Use the information to answer these questions.

1. Who may cash this check? _____

2. Who authorized (signed) this check? _____

3. What is the check amount? _____

4. What is the bank number? _____

5. What is the check number? _____

6. What is the check date? _____

7. How many days does Joan have to cash this check? _____

8. Could Joan cash this check on May 15? _____

9. Could Joan cash this check on February 3? _____

10. Where does Joan work? _____

11. What is the company's address? _____

12. What is Joan's address? _____

13. With what bank does Gerbers & Wilson have an account? _____

Words on a Paycheck Stub

The other half of your paycheck is the *paycheck stub.* Tear off the stub and keep it with your records. The paycheck stub has information that you need to know.

Gerbers & Wilson, Architects • BERLIN, MD 21811							CHECK NO. 90877	
EMPLOYEE NO.	REGULAR	OVERTIME	HOLIDAY	SPECIAL	REGULAR	VACATION		SICK
6752	40.00h				$480.00			
SOCIAL SECURITY NO.	VACATION	SICK	TOTAL	OVERTIME	HOLIDAY		SPECIAL	GROSS PAY
214-32-3420								$480.00
FICA	STATE WITH	CITY WITH	HEALTH INS.	LIFE INS.			TOTAL DEDUCTIONS	
36.00	34.08	0.00	14.45	4.75			$19.20	
FEDERAL WITH		TOTAL TAXES					TOTAL DED & TAX	
72.48		142.56					$161.76	
YEAR-TO-DATE								
GROSS	FICA	FED. WITH TAX	ST. WITH TAX					NET PAY
1440.00	108.00	217.44	102.24					$318.24
PLEASE DETACH BEFORE DEPOSITING CHECK							PAY PERIOD 1/23/96	

Words to Know

gross pay	the total amount you earned
net pay	the amount of the check after deductions; take-home pay
FICA	Federal Insurance Contributions Act tax (or Social Security tax)
withholding (with)	a tax that the employer takes out of your gross pay and sends to the government
deductions	money taken out of your gross pay
pay period	the time period for which you are paid

■ Use the information on the paycheck stub above to answer these questions.

1. What was Joan's gross pay? _____

2. What was Joan's take-home pay? _____

3. Add up all five of Joan's deductions. Write in the total amount. _____

4. How much does Joan's health insurance cost her? _____

5. How much does Joan pay for her life insurance? _____

6. How much did the employer withhold for federal taxes? _____

Job Talk

When you get a job, there are new words to learn. Many of these words relate to your benefits. *Benefits* are advantages that are provided for workers in addition to salary.

salary or wages	money you earn at a job
group health insurance	a health insurance plan for a group of workers. Group insurance is less expensive than individual insurance. Often, the employer pays part of the cost as a company benefit.
workers' compensation	an insurance plan that pays if you are injured at work. The insurance pays for medical costs. If you cannot work, it also pays part of your wages until you are well.
unemployment insurance	insurance that pays you a certain amount of money for a period of time if you lose your job
pension or retirement fund	a fund from which regular payments are made to retired workers if they meet certain requirements, which may include age and length of service

Ask about benefits when you apply for a job. The kinds of benefits offered are one thing to consider when taking a job. Other important considerations are: type of work, salary, working conditions, and advancement opportunities.

Read the information above. Then answer the questions below.

1. Which kind of insurance will help you if you are hurt at work?

_____

2. What do you call the money you receive for working?

_____ or _____

3. Which kind of insurance will help you if you lose your job?

_____

4. Which kind of insurance will help you if you become ill or need an operation?

_____

5. Name three reasons besides salary or benefits for choosing a job.
   Circle the reason that is most important to you.

_____

_____

_____

Vocabulary Builder

Use your knowledge of root words to build your vocabulary. Study each group of words. Then use each word in a sentence.

Root word: Old English *neah,* meaning "nigh" or "near"

neighbor   someone who lives near you
neighborhood   a community; people who live near one another
neighborly   friendly or helpful

1. neighbor _____

2. neighborhood _____

3. neighborly _____

Root word: Latin *senex,* meaning "old"

senate   a group of people who make laws. In ancient Rome, the first members of the Senate came from the oldest and richest families.
senator   a member of a lawmaking branch of government
senatorial   an adjective describing anything related to the senate or a senator

4. senate _____

5. senator _____

6. senatorial _____

Prefix: Latin *im-,* meaning "in"
Root word: Latin *plicare,* meaning "to fold"

employ   to give someone a job; to keep someone busy
employee   a person who works for another person or a company
employer   a person who gives someone a job
employment   work or occupation
employable   physically and mentally fit for work
unemployed   out of work

7. employ _____

8. employee _____

9. employer _____

10. employment _____

11. employable _____

12. unemployed _____

Review Units 4–6

A Write the time shown on each clock in words. Write each time in two different ways.

1. _____

2. _____

3. _____

4. _____

B Complete each sentence.

1. In a _____, February has 29 days.

2. A _____ lasts 100 years.

3. The mayor cancelled the council's _____ meeting. (once a week)

C Choose a word from the list to complete each sentence below.

bold   high-strung   low-calorie   ravenous   blue blood   blue law

1. John did not eat lunch, so he was _____ by dinnertime.

2. The _____ racehorse panicked and threw its rider.

3. All of the restaurants were closed Sunday because of the _____.

D Match each English word with its original language or language group.

1. _____ carnival   a. French

2. _____ alligator   b. Hindi

3. _____ check   c. Italian

4. _____ beef   d. Arabic

5. _____ shampoo   e. Spanish

E Match each item in Column 1 with the correct definition in Column 2.

1. _____ résumé   a. total amount earned during a pay period

2. _____ reference   b. official educational history

3. _____ transcript   c. person who will recommend you to someone else

4. _____ gross pay   d. Social Security tax

5. _____ FICA   e. summary of work and educational experience

Medical Doctors

What is an M.D.? An *M.D.* is a "doctor of medicine," someone who has a doctoral degree in medicine. M.D.'s must have a license to practice medicine from the state in which they work. They must pass an examination to receive this license. Medical doctors are also called *physicians.* Physicians who provide general medical care are called *general practitioners. Specialists* are doctors with special skills in particular areas of medicine.

Specialist	Area of Specialization
allergist	diagnosis and treatment of allergies, asthma, etc.
cardiologist	diseases and injuries related to the heart
dermatologist	diseases and injuries related to the skin
gastroenterologist	illnesses related to the stomach and intestines
gynecologist	diseases and disorders of the female reproductive organs
internist	diagnosis and nonsurgical treatment of diseases
neurologist	diseases and disorders of the nervous system
obstetrician	the care of women during pregnancy and childbirth
ophthalmologist	functions and diseases of the eyes
orthopedic surgeon	treatment of bone injuries and diseases
pediatrician	the care of infants and children
radiologist	diagnosis and treatment of disorders using X rays
surgeon	surgical treatment of disease or injury

Decide which of the doctors listed above you would visit or call in the following situations. Write the name of this doctor on the line.

1. broken arm _____

2. stomach ulcers _____

3. severe rash _____

4. rapid heartbeat _____

5. bad hay fever _____

6. sore throat _____

7. an eye injury _____

8. ruptured appendix _____

9. numbness in hands _____

More Health Problems to Solve

A Match each health situation with the appropriate specialist.

Health Situation	Specialist
1. _____ needs a physical exam to play basketball	**a.** dermatologist
2. _____ pregnancy	**b.** internist
3. _____ needs an X ray	**c.** obstetrician
4. _____ blurred vision	**d.** radiologist
5. _____ severe sunburn	**e.** ophthalmologist

➤ The suffix *-ology* means "the science of."
➤ The suffixes *-ist* and *-ician* mean "a person who works in a particular field."
➤ The suffixes *-iatrics* and *-iatry* mean "medical treatment."

B Match the medical specialty with the name of the medical doctor.

1. _____ dermatology	**a.** cardiologist	
2. _____ neurology	**b.** dermatologist	
3. _____ radiology	**c.** neurologist	
4. _____ allergy	**d.** pediatrician	
5. _____ podiatry	**e.** radiologist	
6. _____ pediatrics	**f.** allergist	
7. _____ cardiology	**g.** podiatrist	

C Find the root words in the new words below. Use that information to help you figure out the meanings.

1. _____ dermatitis	**a.** related to the eye
2. _____ surgical	**b.** related to the inner body
3. _____ internal	**c.** a disease of the skin
4. _____ ophthalmic	**d.** use of X rays to examine inner structure of objects
5. _____ gastritis	**e.** related to surgery
6. _____ radioscopy	**f.** a disease of the stomach

Other Health Professionals

In addition to physicians, there are many other kinds of health care professionals. Although some of these specialists may receive doctoral degrees, they are not medical doctors.

Professional	Specialty
chiropractor	muscle or nerve problems, often in the back
dietitian	preparation of menus for people on special diets
optician	grinding lenses for glasses
optometrist	visual problems and prescriptions for glasses
physical therapist	treatment of injury by exercise, massage, or other physical means
podiatrist	care and treatment of feet
registered nurse (R.N.)	care of sick people, often in hospitals

Fill in the blank with a word that completes each statement.

1. Podiatry is the science that deals with care of the _____.

2. Savita asked the _____ to prepare new lenses for her glasses.

3. Grady needed to be on a salt-free diet, so he talked to a _____.

4. Maria went to an _____ to have her eyes checked.

5. Optometry is the science dealing with problems of the _____.

6. A _____ helped Paula regain the use of her hand after the accident.

7. A _____ cared for Mr. Mason in his home after his heart attack.

8. Wanda visited a _____ to get advice about special shoes.

9. Joe received treatment from a _____ for his back problems.

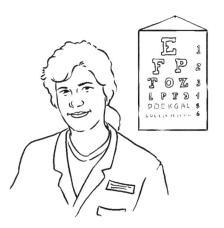

Dentists

The Latin root word *dent* means "tooth." *Dentistry* is the "study of teeth." Dentists care for and treat diseases of the teeth, jaws, mouth, and *gums* (soft tissue around the teeth). There are many interesting words related to the field of dentistry.

Word	Part of Speech	Meaning
dental	adjective	related to teeth
dental floss	noun	a special thread used to clean between the teeth
denture	noun	artificial tooth or set of teeth
dentifrice	noun	product, often a paste, used for cleaning teeth
dentin	noun	the hard tissue under the enamel of a tooth
dentist	noun	a professional person who cares for and repairs teeth
dental hygienist	noun	a person who cleans and examines teeth and gums

➤ **orthodontics**   *Ortho* is a Greek root word meaning "straight or correct." *Odont* is a Greek root word meaning "tooth."

  Orthodontics is "the branch of dentistry dealing with making teeth straight."
  An *orthodontist* is a specialist in straightening crooked teeth.

➤ **periodontics**   *Peri-* is a Greek prefix meaning "around" or "near."

  Periodontics is "the branch of dentistry dealing with the bone and tissue (gums) around the teeth."
  A *periodontist* is a specialist in treating gum disease.

Fill in the blanks with a word that completes each statement.

1. Carla went to her _____ to have her teeth examined.

2. The dentist told her to use _____ to clean between her teeth.

3. Each day Carla uses _____, including toothpaste and mouthwash.

4. The _____ cleaned and examined Carla's teeth.

5. An _____ put braces on Carla's teeth to straighten them.

6. "You'll probably need to visit a _____ someday to treat your gums," said the dentist, "if you don't use dental floss."

7. "If you lose your teeth, you'll need to have _____."

More about Teeth

bicuspid	The Latin prefix *bi-* means "two." *Cuspid* means "pointed." Adults usually have eight *bicuspids*, or teeth with two-pointed crowns.
molar	The Latin root word *mola* means "millstone." *Molars* are the back teeth that we use for grinding food.
incisor	The Latin root word *cis* means "to cut." *Incisors* are the sharp front teeth that we use for biting.
canines	The Latin word *canis* means "dog." *Canine* teeth are the four sharp-pointed teeth that we use for tearing food.
cavity	The Latin word *cavus* means "cave." A *cavity* is a hollow place, such as a hole in a tooth.

A Use the meanings of the root or base words to figure out the meanings of the new words.

1. _____ premolar   **a.** a cut or gash

2. _____ canid   **b.** a member of the animal family that includes dogs

3. _____ cavitation   **c.** a point

4. _____ incision   **d.** the forming of small holes in a body organ or tissue

5. _____ cusp   **e.** tooth in front of a molar

B Fill in the blank with the correct word related to teeth or to dentistry.

denture   canine   cavity   toothbrush   orthodontist
dentifrice   incisors   gums   molars   dentin

1. We use our _____ to grind food.

2. People often chip their front teeth, which we call _____.

3. Our _____ teeth are best for tearing food.

4. I wonder why we do not call a _____ a dental brush?

5. Toothpaste is the most commonly used _____.

6. A hole in a tooth is called a _____.

7. Our _____ are the muscle and tissue that hold our teeth in place.

Pharmaceuticals

The Greek root word *pharmakon* means "drug." The root word *drogue* comes from Old French.

Pharmakon	Drogue	Meaning in English
pharmaceutical	drug	medicine
pharmacist	druggist	a person trained to prepare and dispense drugs
pharmacy	drugstore	a store where you can buy medicines

Other Special Vocabulary

➤ **prescription**   The prefix *pre-* means "before" and the root word *script* means "writing." A *prescription* is a doctor's written instructions for preparing and taking a particular medicine.

➤ **dose**   The measured amount of a medication to be taken at one time.

➤ **side effects**   Additional effects of a drug treatment that are usually unwanted.

➤ **drug interaction**   Reaction that may occur when two or more drugs are taken together.

A Explain the meaning of the following words. Use a dictionary if you need help.

1. Pharmacology_____

2. Pharmaceutical_____

B Fill in the blanks with appropriate words. Answers may vary.

1. The doctor wrote John a _____ for medicine.

2. John went to a _____ to get the medicine.

3. He asked the _____ if the medicine had any side effects.

4. "When should I take this _____?" asked John.

5. It is important to take only the recommended _____ of a medication.

6. Another word for pharmacy is _____.

7. Another word for druggist is _____.

Anatomy

Anatomy is the study of the structures of the bodies of living things.

Our bodies contain many organs. An *organ* is a body part with a special purpose. Organs are made up of *tissue* consisting of specialized cells and other material. When we go to a doctor, it is helpful to know the names of our organs and what they do.

➤ **heart**   a muscular organ that circulates blood throughout our bodies. A heart is like a pump. It makes a thumping or ticking sound. Slang words for the heart are *ticker* and *pump.*

➤ **stomach**   the organ that temporarily stores the food you eat and partly digests it. When we eat a lot, we say our stomachs are *full;* when we are hungry, we say they are *empty.* When we eat food that does not agree with us, we get *indigestion.* The pain of indigestion sometimes feels like a burning near the heart. We call this pain *heartburn.*

➤ **liver**   a large and important organ that helps us digest our food. The liver secretes bile, which helps in the digestion of fats. Diseases of the liver are often very serious.

➤ **lungs**   a pair of very large organs that take in air, send oxygen from the air through the body via the blood, and rid the body of carbon dioxide. When people shout *at the top of their lungs,* they are yelling. The word *lung* comes from the Greek word *lunge,* which means "light in weight." Smoking cigarettes is very bad for the lungs.

Match each word to its meaning.

1. _____ organ
2. _____ liver
3. _____ tissue
4. _____ oxygen
5. _____ carbon dioxide
6. _____ lunge
7. _____ heart
8. _____ ticker

a. a gas that passes out of our lungs when we breathe

b. a Greek word meaning "light in weight"

c. an organ that secretes bile and helps the body digest fats

d. an element in the air that human beings need to live

e. a slang word for "heart"

f. a body part with a special purpose (for example, a heart or a liver)

g. a muscular organ that pumps blood

h. cells and other material that make up an organ

On the Surface

One of the most interesting words in our language is the little word *skin.* It comes from an old German word, *schint,* which means "fruit peel."

➤ **skin**   Skin covers our bodies. We say people are *thick-skinned* when they are not easily offended. The expression *skin-deep* means "on the surface."

The skin's outer layer is called the *epidermis.* The Greek root *derm* means "skin." The middle layer of skin is called the *dermis.* Below the dermis is the *subcutaneous tissue.* In our skin, there are hair follicles, sweat glands, and blood vessels. Our skin is a very interesting subject to explore and to talk about.

➤ **complexion**   The color, appearance, and general condition of the skin, especially on the face.

The word *skin* appears in many phrases and sayings of American English.

■ Explain the meanings of these expressions. Use a dictionary if you need help.

1. Some people think that beauty is only *skin-deep.*

_____

2. Tommy is *thick-skinned.*

_____

3. He got away *by the skin of his teeth.*

_____

4. That's *no skin off my nose!*

_____

5. Eunice is very *thin-skinned.*

_____

6. Randy tried to *save his own skin.*

_____

7. "Mom will *skin us alive* if we are late again," said Annie to her brother.

_____

8. "Sam really *gets under my skin.*"

_____

Vocabulary Builder

We often refer to the parts of the body in phrases and sayings. Look at the following examples.

■ Study the definition and the example. Then, use the word or phrase in a sentence of your own.

1. **Brainstorm**—(verb) to allow ideas to flow freely; (noun) a sudden good idea
   The club officers met to *brainstorm* ideas about projects for the year.

2. **Brainwash**—to try to change someone's basic beliefs and ideas
   Ronny said, "Those TV commercials have *brainwashed* you."

3. **Brain wave**—a sudden, unusually good idea; similar to brainstorm
   LaDonna had a *brain wave* about how to solve her problem.

4. **Take it to heart**—to take something very seriously
   Ralph *took to heart* the coach's advice and began to practice every day.

5. **From one's heart**—being very sincere
   I am sending you this message *from my heart.*

6. **Heart and soul**—completely
   Maria and Luis loved their child *heart and soul.*

7. **Heartache**—sadness
   The loss of her best friend caused Anya much *heartache.*

8. **Have a heart**—slang expression meaning "to be kind"
   "*Have a heart,* Mom. Let me have the car tonight, please."

9. **Get on someone's nerves**—to make someone nervous or upset
   Paul's little brother *got on his nerves.*

UNIT 7 *MEDICAL TALK*   59

Kinds of Insurance

Insurance provides protection against the loss of valuable things. An *insurance policy* is a contract with an insurance company that guarantees that the company will repay you for a loss. There are many kinds of insurance.

Kind of Insurance	When the Insurance Pays
Automobile insurance	• You injure someone in a car accident; • You damage someone else's car while driving; • Someone steals or damages your car; • You are injured by an uninsured driver.
Life insurance	• The insured person dies; • The insured person borrows against the cash value of the policy; • The insured person gives up the policy and receives the cash value. (Note: Not all policies accumulate a cash value.)
Health insurance	• You have doctor or hospital expenses; • You receive emergency medical treatment.
Homeowner's insurance	• Your home or property is damaged or destroyed; • Your personal belongings are damaged or stolen; • Someone is injured on your property.

An *insurance company* is a business that issues insurance policies.
The person who buys the policy is called the *insured* or the *policyholder.*
The insurance company charges a fee for the policy called a *premium.*

■ Which kind of insurance is needed in each of these situations?
Write the correct letter on the line provided.

A. Life insurance **C.** Automobile insurance
B. Health insurance **D.** Homeowner's insurance

_____ 1. Mr. and Mrs. Burack want to provide money for their children if they die before their children are grown.

_____ 2. Fred went into the hospital to have an operation.

_____ 3. Someone stole Stefani's car.

_____ 4. A tree fell down in the Conways' yard and damaged their fence.

_____ 5. Erica is going to have a baby.

_____ 6. Burglars broke into Melva's house and stole her antique furniture.

Talking about Auto Insurance

Automobile insurance policies provide *coverage* for different kinds of problems.

Kinds of Auto Insurance Coverage

comprehensive	This covers damage caused by fire, theft, and vandalism. The insurance company pays any expenses in addition to the *deductible*, the amount the policyholder has agreed to pay for damages.
collision	This covers damage to your own car in an accident. The insurance company pays any expense beyond the deductible.
property damage liability	When you damage someone else's property with your car, your insurance pays to repair the other car or property.
bodily injury liability	When you injure another person in an accident that you caused, your insurance pays for the medical treatment of that person.

Other Words to Know

➤ **liability**   the amount of money you are legally responsible to pay for injury to other people or for damage to their property

➤ **limits of liability**   the maximum amount that your insurance company will pay for each accident or injured person

➤ **deductible**   the amount you agree to pay for each accident before your insurance coverage begins

Which kind of insurance do you need in each situation? Write the correct letter on the line provided.

A. Comprehensive   **C.** Property damage liability
B. Collision   **D.** Bodily injury liability

_____ **1.** You are parking your car. You accidentally hit another car and damage it. Your car is not damaged.

_____ **2.** You cause a car accident. Another person is injured and requires medical care.

_____ **3.** You back into a fire hydrant and damage your car. The hydrant is not damaged.

_____ **4.** Your car goes out of control and knocks down a fence in someone's yard.

_____ **5.** Someone steals your car.

_____ **6.** You cause a traffic accident. You damage only your car.

_____ **7.** A fire in your neighbor's house burns your car.

_____ **8.** An uninsured driver causes an accident in which your car is damaged.

Talking about Life Insurance

Life insurance provides money for family members or other people after we die.

Basic Kinds of Life Insurance

whole life	provides coverage for the lifetime of the insured. When you die, the insurance company pays your beneficiary the amount for which you were insured. With some policies, if you live past a certain age, you no longer have to pay the premium, or the amount you pay may be less.
term life	provides benefits only for a certain period. You may be able to renew the policy when it expires, but the premiums will *increase* as you get older.

Words to Know

➤ **premium**   the fee you pay for insurance

➤ **insured**   the person whom the policy insures

➤ **beneficiary** the person who benefits when you die; the person who collects the insurance

➤ **policy**   the written contract between the insured person and the insurance company

Other Facts About Life Insurance

➤ The cost of the insurance (the premium) depends on your age.

➤ The younger you are when you take out a policy, the *lower* your premium will be.

➤ The more insurance you have, the *higher* the premium.

➤ An *insurance agent* represents the insurance company and sells you a policy.

■ Answer these questions about life insurance.

1. Why do people buy life insurance? _____

_____

2. The policy is the _____ between the policyholder and the insurance company.

3. A person who sells insurance policies is an _____.

4. What is a premium? _____

5. Which kind of insurance provides coverage for your entire lifetime?

_____

6. The cost of life insurance depends mainly on two things:

   (a) _____ and (b) _____

Talking about Health Insurance

Health insurance helps pay medical bills. There are several types of health insurance.

Comprehensive major medical expense insurance pays for medical and hospital expenses; usually includes costs of hospital room, meals, medicines, doctors' fees, medical examinations, emergency care, laboratory tests, X rays, and surgery.

Hospital expense insurance provides a fixed payment to cover a certain number of days of hospitalization each year, including fees for surgery, tests, X rays, and other services.

Surgical expense insurance covers the fee, or part of the fee, for an operation.

Outpatient expense insurance pays for nonsurgical treatment, X rays, and tests.

Alternative Health Care Programs

➤ A *medical service plan* makes direct payments to the doctor or hospital that provided the medical care.

➤ A *health maintenance organization (HMO)* provides almost complete health care services for a flat fee. The HMO tells you which hospital to go to. It has doctors for you to visit for other medical care.

Other Words to Know

➤ **co-payment**   the part of a medical bill (over the amount of the deductible) to be paid by the policyholder

➤ **deductible**   the amount you pay before your insurance coverage begins

➤ **limit**   the maximum amount the insurance company will pay for treatment of a particular illness

➤ **restrictions**   medical problems or expenses that your insurance does not cover (for example, some policies do not cover dental and eye care expenses)

Answer these questions about health insurance.

1. What does HMO stand for? _____

2. Your doctor bill is $80.00. The deductible is $50.00. You must pay

_____.

3. Are X rays paid for by comprehensive major medical insurance? _____

4. Do all comprehensive major medical plans pay for eye examinations? _____

5. Does an HMO cover most medical expenses for a flat fee? _____

6. You belong to an HMO. Can you usually go to any doctor of your choice? _____

Vocabulary Builder

Goodness! Gracious! Sakes Alive!
These words and expressions all contain the word *good.* Add them to your vocabulary.

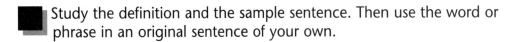 Study the definition and the sample sentence. Then use the word or phrase in an original sentence of your own.

1. **Good-humored**—cheerful and agreeable; pleasant
   Juanita is a good-humored person.

2. **Good-hearted**—kind and generous
   Because Mickey is so good-hearted, he helped his little brother with his homework.

3. **Good-for-nothing**—worthless; useless
   "Fred is a good-for-nothing rascal," said his aunt.

4. **For good**—permanently; forever
   We were sad to learn that the theatre is closed for good.

5. **Come to no good**—come to a bad end; end in failure
   We knew that project would come to no good from the very beginning.

6. **To the good**—helpful; for the best
   Cheryl's efforts to raise money for the library were all to the good.

7. **Good-looking**—handsome; pleasant in appearance
   The winner of the dog show was a good-looking terrier.

8. **Good-natured**—having a pleasant disposition; easy to get along with
   "My sister Suzie is very good-natured," Dan said.

9. **A good turn**—a good deed; a friendly, helpful act; a favor
   The baby-sitter did the children a good turn by helping them learn to spell.

What Is Real Estate?

Real estate refers to land, its natural features, and structures built on it. We use many different words to describe real estate.

Everyone needs a place to live. Your main choices are to *buy* a house or condominium or to *rent* a house or an apartment.

Types of Real Estate

apartment	a group of rooms in an apartment building that includes a kitchen and bathroom. An apartment may also be part of a house.
unit	a living space—such as an apartment—that is part of a larger building
condominium	an individually owned unit in a multiunit building
single-family home	a house built for one family
duplex	a house containing two separate units

Other Words to Know

➤ **lot**　　a piece of land; a plot of ground

➤ **property**　　something a person owns: a house, condominium, or specific piece of land

➤ **residence**　　the place where a person lives

➤ **rental unit**　　a unit that someone rents; usually an apartment

Match each word in Column 1 with its definition in Column 2.

Column 1	Column 2
1. _____ duplex	**a.** where you live
2. _____ lot	**b.** an individually owned unit in a multiunit building
3. _____ unit	**c.** a part of a larger building
4. _____ property	**d.** group of rooms with a kitchen and bathroom
5. _____ residence	**e.** something you own
6. _____ condominium	**f.** a house containing two units
7. _____ apartment	**g.** plot of land

Signing a Lease

When you rent an apartment or a house, you usually sign a contract called a *lease.* Always read any contract that you sign very carefully. You might want to discuss it with a lawyer.

➤ **lease**   (noun) an agreement to rent a house or apartment for a certain period of time; or (verb) to rent a house or apartment

➤ **rent**   (noun) the amount of money paid to use a house or apartment; or (verb) to lease a house or apartment

➤ **tenant**   a person who rents a piece of property

➤ **landlord**   an owner of property who leases the property to other people

A Fill in the blanks with the correct words.

1. After Sam graduated from high school, he decided to _____ an apartment.

2. The _____ each month was $450.

3. When he rented the apartment, Sam became a _____.

4. Sam and the landlord signed a _____ before he moved in.

When you rent an apartment, you need to provide the landlord with certain information.

credit reference   —name of a bank, credit card company, or individual who has loaned you money in the past

personal reference —someone who knows you personally, such as a neighbor, a teacher, or a friend

name of employer   —the company or person for whom you work

current residence   —the address of the place where you now live, before you move into the new apartment

B Fill in the blank with a word that completes each sentence.

1. Before Sam signed the lease, the _____ asked him to complete an application.

2. Sam listed his bank as a credit _____.

3. He listed his neighbor as a _____ reference.

4. The name of his _____ is Barnes Department Store.

5. Sam's current _____ is at 3601 Westley Lane.

Money Talk

When you buy a house, you will need to understand words about money.

loan	money that is borrowed
debt	money that is owed
loan payment	money used to pay back a loan, usually in the form of monthly installments
principal	the amount of money loaned
interest	a fee you pay for a loan, usually a percentage of the principal
property tax	money you pay to the government when you own property
insurance	protects against loss by fire or theft. You must have homeowner's insurance to apply for a home loan.
note	a written promise to pay back a debt
down payment	a partial payment on a house, car, or other property
deed	a document that shows that you own a piece of property

Fill in the blanks with the word that completes each sentence.

1. Sam's sister Laura applied for a _____ at a bank to buy a house.

2. She made a _____ of $8,000 on the house.

3. The _____ due on the loan was eight percent.

4. Every month, Laura makes a _____ by sending a check to her bank.

5. Laura had to sign a _____ that stated her promise to repay the loan.

6. As a property owner, Laura has to pay a property _____ to the government.

7. Laura's _____ was the amount of her loan.

8. The money she borrowed became a _____ that she owes.

9. The legal document that shows that Laura owns her house is a _____.

10. Laura's homeowner's _____ protects her in case she has a fire that damages her home.

Word History

Condominium comes from the Latin prefix *com-*, which means "with," and from the Latin word *dominium,* which means "ownership."

Duplex is a Latin word meaning "double."

We rely on electric energy to light and heat our homes. Here are some words that relate to our electric power supply.

electric current	the flow of electric charges (electrons) in a substance
electric power	electric energy that is used to do work; provides energy for light and heat and for many appliances, such as stoves and vacuum cleaners
power plant	produces huge amounts of electric power for customers by using steam or flowing water to drive electric generators
electric generator	a machine that changes mechanical energy from steam or flowing water to electric energy
electric circuit	the path followed by electric current between the source of electric energy and an output device, such as a lamp or motor
electric switch	a device that controls the flow of electric current in a circuit; turning on a switch completes a circuit and allows current to flow through; turning off the switch breaks the circuit and stops the flow of current
electric meter	a device that measures electric current; used by electric utility companies to measure the amount of energy used by customers

The following words describe devices that use electric energy to produce light.

➤ **light bulb**   a device that changes electric energy to light; types of light bulbs or tubes include incandescent, fluorescent, and neon

➤ **incandescent**   a type of light bulb that contains a filament (wire) that gives off light when it is heated by electric current flowing through it

➤ **fluorescent**   a type of light bulb or tube containing gases that give off energy when electric current flows through them; the energy causes a special coating inside the tube to give off light

➤ **neon**   a type of light bulb that contains neon gas, which gives off red light when electric current passes through it; bright colors in neon signs come from neon combined with other gases or from colored tubes

Complete each sentence below.

1. The filament inside an _____ light bulb gives off light.

2. Large _____ supply electric power to millions of customers.

3. An electric generator changes _____ to electric energy.

4. At home, we use _____ to turn on lamps.

5. An electric switch controls the flow of electric _____ in a circuit.

6. An _____ shows the amount of electric power used in a home.

7. _____ light bulbs contain a special coating that gives off light.

Computers and Their Parts

Computers are everywhere. These machines perform complicated calculations with great speed and store huge amounts of information. They can be *programmed* (instructed) to do many tasks.

microprocessor	a chip containing an electronic circuit that controls a computer
embedded computer	microprocessor used to control the workings of many different kinds of machines, from coffee makers to automobiles
personal computer	a small computer for use by one person at a time; may be a desktop, laptop, or palmtop computer; usually contains a microprocessor
mainframe computer	a large computer that can solve very complicated problems and store huge amounts of information; a mainframe computer can be used by more than one person at a time
keyboard	set of keys with which information can be entered into a computer
monitor	a screen that shows information being entered into a computer with the keyboard and mouse or that shows results of the computer's work
mouse	a small, handheld device used to enter commands into a computer
disk drive	a part of a computer that can read information recorded on a magnetic disk, such as a floppy disk
floppy disk	a flexible disk on which information can be magnetically encoded so that a computer can read it
central processing unit	the part of the computer—often a single microprocessor—that actually performs work on information entered into the computer; (abbreviation: **CPU**)

■ Complete each sentence below.

1. The _____ computer in my watch is a _____.

2. The results of the work done by the computer's _____ could be seen

   on the _____.

3. You can type information into a computer on a _____, or you can use

   a handheld device called a _____ to enter commands.

4. The computer read information from a _____ placed

   in the _____ drive.

5. A _____ can be used by many people at the same time; a

   _____ can be used by one person at a time.

Storing Information

There are a number of ways to store *data* (information) on a computer.

transistor	tiny electronic device that controls the flow of electric current in a computer; transistors are the main components in microprocessors and memory chips
memory	the part of the computer that stores data and programs currently in use by the computer
memory chip	a system of circuits, wires, and transistors that stores information within a computer
hard disk	a storage device built into a computer that can store huge amounts of information for long periods
random-access memory	the memory contained on magnetic disks and tapes; it is called "random-access" because the data stored there can be easily searched or replaced; (abbreviation: **RAM**)
read-only memory	information stored in a way such that the computer cannot change it; ROM units include compact discs (CD-ROM), cartridges, and silicon chips; (abbreviation: **ROM**)
CD-ROM	compact disc read-only memory; a CD-ROM can store the information contained in thousands of printed pages; CD-ROMs can also store pictures and sound; CD-ROMs require special players

Complete each sentence below.

1. A computer's _____ stores only information currently being used by the computer.

2. A built-in storage device for storing data for very long periods is called a

   _____.

3. _____ memory contains data that can be easily searched and replaced.

4. The flow of electric current in a microprocessor is controlled by _____.

5. Special players are needed to read _____.

6. CD-ROM is a type of _____ memory.

7. James has stored large amounts of _____ on the

   _____ of his computer.

8. The data stored in _____ can be easily changed;

   however, a computer cannot change data stored in _____.

Computer Data

The word *data* simply means "information" or "facts." It is the plural form of the Latin root word *datum*, which means "something known." *Computer data* are bits of information in a form that a computer can use. Listed below are words that are used to describe computer data.

➤ **binary numeration system** — the system of numbers used to encode all of the information entered into a computer; all numbers in the binary system are represented by only only two digits, 0 and 1; when data are recorded on a disk, these digits are represented by tiny magnets pointing in opposite directions

➤ **digit** — an element that, by itself or in combination with others, forms numbers in a numeration system

➤ **bit** — a digit in a binary number system, either a 0 or a 1; the smallest unit of information a computer can process

➤ **byte** — a group of bits, usually eight, that a computer can read or compute all at once

➤ **kilobyte** — a term used to represent the capacity of a computer's memory; a kilobyte is roughly equal to 1,000 bytes

➤ **megabyte** — another term used to represent the capacity of a computer's memory; a megabyte is roughly equal to 1,000,000 bytes

Fill in the blank with a word that completes each sentence.

1. _____ are elements that are used to represent numbers in any numeration system.

2. A kilobyte is roughly equal to _____ bytes.

3. Eight _____ make up a byte.

4. A _____ is roughly equal to 1,000 kilobytes.

5. In the binary numeration system, there are only _____ digits.

   They are _____ and _____ .

6. The smallest unit of information that a computer can process is

   called a _____ .

7. The _____ system is used to encode information so that a computer can process or store it.

Software Talk

Hardware refers to the computer equipment. *Software* refers to the programs that run the computer. A computer program is a set of instructions that tells the computer what to do. Computer programs are available that make many kinds of work (accounting, word processing, and database management, for example) easier to do on a computer.

A Decide whether each item is hardware or software. Circle your answer.

1. a hard disk   hardware or software

2. an accounting program   hardware or software

3. a computer monitor   hardware or software

4. a printer   hardware or software

5. a database management system   hardware or software

An *application* is a way that we use a computer. Here are some common computer applications.

➤ **word processing**   a computer program that turns a computer into an electronic typewriter. Words appear on the monitor as you type on the keyboard and can be easily changed or deleted. To get a *hard copy* (paper copy) of what you have typed, you must have a printer.

➤ **accounting**   a computer program that keeps records of expenses and income. Businesses need accounting programs. People also use accounting programs on their personal computers at home.

➤ **database management**   important types of computer software which are used to store information and to print special kinds of reports. These kinds of software manage lists of names and addresses, company records, and other data.

B Use the information above to answer these questions.

Which kind of software would you use:

1. To keep records of the money you earn, spend, and save?

   _____

2. To write a letter or a report?

   _____

3. To create a file with all of your customers' names and addresses?

   _____

Vocabulary Builder

A *transistor* is a tiny device that controls the flow of electric charges in almost all kinds of electronic equipment. The word *transistor* is a combination of parts of two other words, *trans*fer and re*sistor*, and was first used in 1948.

Trans- is a prefix meaning "through," "across," or "beyond."

You will find this prefix in many words.

transatlantic	across the Atlantic Ocean, such as a *transatlantic* plane flight
transfer	to carry something from one place to another
transform	to change something to a new form; to make over
transit	passage from one place to another; *in transit* means "in motion"
translate	to change from one language to another
transmit	to send something, such as a message, from one person to another
transpacific	across the Pacific Ocean
transplant	to completely move from one place to another; to relocate
transport	to move or carry freight from one place to another
transpose	to change the order of items in a group; to switch places

Fill in the blank with the correct word.

1. Fred _____ the speech from Spanish to English.

2. These bananas were _____ by ship from Panama to the United States.

3. The _____ telephone cable allows people in the United States to talk to friends in Europe.

4. Jackie's new haircut seemed to _____ her appearance completely.

5. When they are four inches tall, we will _____ the herbs to the garden.

6. Mickey _____ his belongings to his new room.

7. When people are in the military, they are often in _____.

8. The Coast Guard _____ weather warnings to ships by radio.

9. The detective noticed that the items on the table had been _____.

10. The invention of the _____ was important in computer science.

11. The prefix *trans-* means "through," "across," or "_____."

12. The quickest way to go from California to Japan is by a _____ flight.

Review Units 7–10

A Write the name of the specialist you would need to see for each health condition. Note: Not every specialist will be an M.D.

1. pregnancy _____

2. gum disease _____

3. questions about medications _____

4. special diets _____

5. back pain _____

B Use items from the list to complete the sentences below.

deductible   lease   whole life insurance   interest   principal
HMO   liability   co-payment   comprehensive   premium

1. Every policyholder pays a fee called a _____ for his or her insurance.

2. _____ auto insurance covers the cost of damage from fire, theft, or vandalism.

3. _____ provides coverage for the entire lifetime of the insured.

4. I liked the apartment and told the landlord I would sign the _____.

5. The fee paid for a loan is called the _____.

C Complete the paragraph below with words from the list.

monitor   disk drive   circuit   keyboard   microprocessor
megabyte   bit   hard disk   data   personal computer
floppy disks   database   mainframe   hardware

Marisa bought a **1.**_____ to use at home. Before she got the computer,

she thought about the different **2.**_____ and software she would need. She

wanted a **3.**_____ and a mouse to enter **4.**_____ into the

computer. She also needed a large **5.**_____ so that she could make drawings on

the screen. Her computer is driven by a **6.**_____, which is tiny

but very powerful; the computer can store a large amount of information on its

7._____. Marisa bought a box of **8.**_____ to use in the

computer's **9.**_____. Each disk can hold one **10.**_____ of data.

Weather Reports

Everybody talks about the weather, but nobody does anything about it.
—Charles D. Warner (1890)

The weather is one of the most popular topics of conversation. So much depends on what is happening outside. Weather is one part of our lives that we have little control over. We must adapt to hot and cold temperatures, to rain and to snow.

Weather Words to Know

atmosphere	the air surrounding the earth; from the Greek words *atmos,* meaning "vapor," and *sphaira,* meaning "sphere"
climate	the average weather conditions in an area over a period of years
forecast	prediction (noun); predict (verb)
humidity	measure of the amount of water vapor in the air
meteorologist	a person who studies weather events and tries to predict weather changes
meteorology	science that deals with weather events and weather forecasting
precipitation	moisture that falls from the clouds as rain, sleet, snow, or hail
temperature	the degree of heat in the atmosphere
weather	the condition of the atmosphere in terms of temperature, precipitation, and wind
wind chill	estimate of how cold the wind makes a person feel

Fill in the blank with a word that completes each statement.

1. The _____ today is delightful!

2. It was a dry summer; there was very little _____.

3. We tuned in to hear the _____ give the daily weather forecast.

4. The _____ in Florida is milder than in Montana.

5. As the sun set and the winds increased, the _____ dropped.

6. The study of weather and climate is called _____.

7. Pollution is causing much damage to our _____.

8. Did the meteorologist _____ rain for Saturday?

9. Our clothes felt damp due to the high _____ in the rain forest.

10. The _____ made us feel much colder.

Listen to the Wind

The wind was a torrent of darkness among the gusty trees.
—Noyes, "The Highwayman"

Who has seen the wind?
Neither you nor I.
But when the trees bow down their heads,
The wind is passing by.
—Christina Rossetti, "Who Has Seen the Wind?"

The wind is "air in motion." Here are some words used to describe moving air.

blast	a violent rush of air; an explosion
breath	air we take into our lungs and then let out; a slight movement of air
breeze	a gentle wind
draft	a current of air that is drawn inside through an opening in a doorway or window
gust	a sudden, strong rush of air
puff	a short, sudden burst of air
squall	a brief, violent windstorm, usually with rain or snow
whiff	a light puff or gust of air

Special Kinds of Winds

➤ **jet stream** a band of high-speed winds that flows from the east or west around the earth or part of the earth

➤ **monsoon** a seasonal wind that blows over the northern Indian Ocean and nearby lands, usually bringing heavy rains in the spring

➤ **trade winds** strong winds that blow steadily toward the equator from the northeast or southeast

➤ **zephyr** the west wind, a gentle breeze; from *Zephyros*, the Greek god of the west wind

Write a sentence using each word.

1. draft _____

2. gust _____

3. monsoon _____

4. squall _____

5. breeze _____

Stormy Weather

Perhaps the most important part of weather forecasting is predicting major storms. Here are some of the types of storms to know about.

blizzard	a severe snowstorm, usually with high, cold winds
cyclone	a system of winds that spirals around a center and has a forward motion. Different kinds of cyclones include hurricanes, typhoons, and tornadoes.
gale	a wind that blows at speeds of 32 to 63 miles per hour (mph)
hurricane	a cyclone with wind speeds of 74 mph or greater that forms in tropical regions of the North Atlantic Ocean or eastern North Pacific Ocean
northeaster	a storm or a strong wind coming from the northeast
norther	a storm or strong wind coming from the north, specifically such a wind in the Gulf of Mexico or the southern United States
storm	any wind whose speed is 64 to 72 mph; also, any disturbance of the atmosphere accompanied by wind and rain, snow, or hail
tornado	a violent windstorm with wind speeds of 200 mph or greater; forms a twisting, funnel-shaped cloud that can be very destructive if it reaches to the ground
typhoon	a storm like a hurricane except that it occurs in the western Pacific Ocean; usually accompanied by heavy rains
whirlwind	a current of air whirling upward in a spiral

Fill in the blanks with a word or phrase that completes each statement.

1. A small _____ picked up leaves and dust in its spiral.

2. Both hurricanes and typhoons are types of _____.

3. A _____ is a funnel-shaped cloud with wind speeds of 200 mph or more.

4. A wind with speeds of 32 to 63 miles per hour is a _____.

5. A tropical storm with winds over 73 miles per hour is a _____.

6. A storm with snow and driving winds is a _____.

7. In a _____, the wind speed is from 64 to 72 miles per hour.

8. The weather reporter warned the people living near the Gulf of Mexico about the possibility of a _____.

9. Much damage is often caused by _____ in countries of the western Pacific Ocean, such as the Philippines.

When the Winds Die Down

After the storm comes the quiet—a time in which the winds die down. There are many words that describe the process of slowing down or becoming less.

abate	to make or to become less in degree or intensity We waited for the storm to *abate* before going back outside.
curtail	to cut short, to shorten We usually *curtail* outdoor activities when the weather is stormy.
diminish	to make or to become smaller in size, degree, or importance The winds *diminished* from 50 to 10 miles an hour.
ebb	to become less; to decline The flood from the typhoon finally *ebbed* away.
lessen	to make or to become less; to decrease; to diminish The wind speeds *lessened* in the afternoon.
reduce	to lessen in amount or size The winds were *reduced* following the storm.
wane	to gradually decrease in extent or degree The strength of the hurricane finally began to *wane*.

A Use the definitions on pages 76, 77, and 78 to solve the crossword puzzle below.

Across

2. to gradually decrease
4. a wind storm
6. a current of air
8. to cut short
9. to lessen or decline
11. a violent, whirling windstorm
13. to become less; to decrease

Down

1. to lessen in amount or size
3. Breeze and wind describe moving ____.
5. to become less in degree or intensity
7. to become smaller in degree, size, or importance
10. a gentle wind
11. opposite of hot
12. air in motion

B Write a paragraph using as many words from the puzzle as you can. Share your paragraph with your classmates.

Vocabulary Builder

There are many words related to *weather.* Here are a few of them.

weather	the condition of the atmosphere, temperature, wind speed, and moisture at a particular time and place
weather-beaten	showing the effects of the weather; worn down by the weather
weather vane	a free-swinging, flat piece of metal mounted on an upright rod that shows which way the wind is blowing; usually placed on the roof of a building
weathercock	a weather vane in the shape of a rooster
weatherproof	protected from the effects of the weather; a weatherproof coat or boots
weather stripping	a strip of material used to cover the joint between a door or window and its frame in order to keep out the wind or cold
weather map	a map or chart showing the condition of the weather in a certain area at a given time

Fill in the blank with a word that completes each sentence.

1. The _____ told us the direction of the wind.

2. To keep out the wind, the Martins put _____ around all their doors and windows.

3. Whether we have our picnic on Saturday depends on the _____.

4. Since George worked outside, he purchased a _____ coat and boots.

5. The picnic table that we kept on our patio became _____ after a few years.

6. We call a weather vane that is in the shape of a rooster a _____.

7. The _____ showed the temperature range across the state.

The *Celsius scale* is a temperature scale that was invented by the Swedish astronomer Anders Celsius in 1742. On a Celsius thermometer, 0° represents the freezing point of water, and 100° is its boiling point. The Celsius scale is also called the *centigrade scale.*

The *Fahrenheit scale* is a temperature scale that was invented by the German physicist Gabriel Daniel Fahrenheit in 1714. On the Fahrenheit scale, 32° is the freezing point of water and 212° is the boiling point.

UNIT 12

The Family Tree

Lesson 1

Many words in the English language describe our family relationships. Look at the family tree below. The plus sign (+) is used to indicate a marriage.

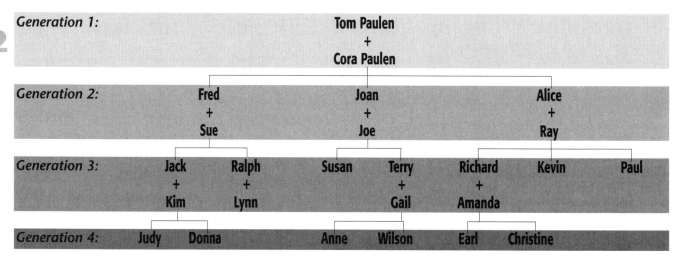

Family Vocabulary

parents	your mother and father
grandparents	the parents of your mother or father
aunt	the sister of your mother or father
uncle	the brother of your mother or father
first cousins	the children of your aunts and uncles
second cousins	the children of your parents' first cousins
spouse	the person you are married to
in-laws	people related to you by marriage, such as a sister-in-law

 Study the family tree above. Then, answer these questions.

1. How are Sue and Joe (Generation 2) related? _____

2. What is the name of Terry and Susan's uncle? _____

3. Jack and Ralph are brothers. How are Kim and Lynn related? _____

4. How many first cousins do Judy and Donna have? _____

5. How many grandchildren do Tom and Cora have? _____

6. How many great-grandchildren do Tom and Cora have? _____

7. How many grandchildren do Fred and Sue have? _____

8. How many children do Alice and Ray have? _____

9. How is Terry related to Richard (Generation 3)? _____

10. How is Susan (Generation 3) related to Anne (Generation 4)? _____

Brothers and Sisters

There are a number of words that describe the relationship among children in the same family.

➤sister   a girl or a woman who has both parents in common with another person

➤brother   a boy or a man who has both parents in common with another person

➤half-brother/half-sister a brother or sister who has one parent in common with another person

➤stepbrother/stepsister a brother or sister whose parent has married the parent of another person. Stepbrothers and stepsisters are related only by marriage.

➤stepmother/stepfather a man or woman who becomes the parent of a child by marrying the child's mother or father. Stepparents and stepchildren are related only by marriage.

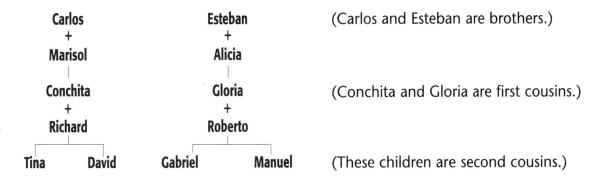

Carlos + **Marisol** | **Conchita** + **Richard**	**Esteban** + **Alicia** | **Gloria** + **Roberto**	(Carlos and Esteban are brothers.) (Conchita and Gloria are first cousins.)
Tina **David**	**Gabriel** **Manuel**	(These children are second cousins.)

A Study the family tree above. Then complete the sentences below.

1. _____ is Conchita's uncle.

2. _____ is Gloria's uncle.

3. Marisol is Gloria's aunt by _____.

4. Gabriel and Manuel are _____.

5. Conchita and Gloria are _____.

6. Tina and Gabriel are _____.

B Write the correct relationship in each sentence below.

Larry and Jonelle got married. Mark is Larry's son. Ricky is Jonelle's son.
Larry and Jonelle had a child together and named her Brenda.

1. Mark and Ricky are _____.

2. Brenda is Mark's _____.

3. Ricky is Brenda's _____.

4. Larry is Brenda's _____.

5. Jonelle is Mark's _____.

Larry
+
Jonelle

Mark **Brenda** **Ricky**

In Our Past

When we talk about our relatives from many generations ago, we need new words.

➤**ancestor** (noun)   a relative who lived before you; usually used to refer to relatives older than your grandparents
The Irish King Brian Boru was one of President Reagan's *ancestors.*

➤**ancestry** (noun)   term used to refer to all of your ancestors together
Bill's *ancestry* is French and Native American.

➤**ancestral** (adjective)   having to do with one's ancestors
Ann and Charles visited their *ancestral* home in West Africa.

A Complete each of the following sentences correctly.

1. My _____ were farmers for hundreds of years.

2. Arturo's family went to visit their _____ home in Sicily.

3. What you do know about your _____?

4. Ranjay's _____ lived in India.

5. Alex Haley wrote about his _____ in the book *Roots.*

6. The families tried to protect their _____ lands in Canada.

When we talk about our heritage, we need new words.

➤**heir** (noun)   person who receives property from someone who has died; person who receives a characteristic from an ancestor

➤**inherit** (verb)   to receive property or some characteristic from an ancestor

➤**heritage** (noun)   something handed down from ancestors, such as a culture or tradition

➤**hereditary** (adjective)   passed down from an ancestor

B Complete each of the following sentences correctly.

1. Hair and eye color are _____ characteristics.

2. We _____ many physical traits from our parents.

3. The boys became interested in their cultural _____.

4. Karin was her grandfather's only _____.

C Write a paragraph describing your ancestry or the ancestry of someone you know. Use six vocabulary words from this unit to describe your relatives. Then circle those six words. Use your own paper.

Lines of Descent

A Fill in the blanks with a word that completes each sentence correctly. There may be more than one correct answer.

➤ **descent** (noun)   ancestry; heritage
➤ **descendant** (noun)   an offspring (child) of a particular ancestor
➤ **descend** (verb)   to come down from a particular ancestor; usually used in the phrase "to be descended from"

Example: One of Mrs. Tyber's *descendants* is a writer.

1. Queen Elizabeth II is _____ from the House of Hanover.

2. Paul hoped all his _____ would be able to attend college.

3. Saaid is of Egyptian _____.

Words Used to Describe Lineage

➤ **lineage**   ancestry; also, descendants of a common ancestor
➤ **clan**   a social group made up of several families who are descended from a common ancestor. The word *clan* comes from the Scottish Gaelic word meaning "offspring."
➤ **genealogy**   the study of family descent; a record of the descent of an individual or group from an ancestor
➤ **forebear**   an ancestor
➤ **offspring**   children; descendants
➤ **progeny**   children, descendants, or offspring
➤ **generation**   one step in the line of descent from an ancestor. A grandfather, son, and granddaughter make up three generations.

B Complete each sentence below.

1. Eileen O'Hara became interested in _____ and drew her family tree.

2. Progeny is another word for _____.

3. Anne Marie's _____ came to Louisiana from Canada.

4. Her family's involvement in politics goes back several _____.

5. The _____ of the Scottish Highlands represented groups of related families.

6. Chris traced his _____ back to an ancient Viking warrior.

UNIT 12

The prefix *fore-* means "before in time, place, or order." There are many words with this prefix. Study the examples below.

➤ **foreman/forewoman**   the head of a group of workers or of a jury

➤ **forebode**   to know or to predict beforehand that something harmful will occur

➤ **foregone**   previous; something already decided; such as a foregone conclusion

A Match the words with their definitions.

1. _____ forearm   **a.** the part of the scene in the front or closest to the viewer

2. _____ forenoon   **b.** the part of the face between the eyebrows and the hairline

3. _____ forewarn   **c.** first in time or place

4. _____ forecast   **d.** the front part of a ship's deck

5. _____ foredeck   **e.** ancestors

6. _____ forebears   **f.** the finger nearest the thumb; the index finger

7. _____ forecourt   **g.** the extreme front

8. _____ foreground   **h.** to predict the future, particularly weather

9. _____ forehead   **i.** the court at the front; in tennis, the court nearest the net

10. _____ foresee   **j.** the part of the arm between the elbow and the wrist

11. _____ foremost   **k.** time between sunrise and noon; morning

12. _____ forepaw   **l.** an animal's front paw

13. _____ forefinger   **m.** anything that serves as a sign of future developments

14. _____ forefront   **n.** to see beforehand

15. _____ forerunner   **o.** to warn ahead of time

B Complete each sentence with one of the words above.

1. The _____ of the jury read the verdict.

2. The Wright brothers' airplane was a _____ of our present-day jets.

3. The weather reporter tried to _____ the public of the coming storm.

4. The puppy limped because his _____ was injured.

5. John Steinbeck was one of the _____ writers of his time.

6. Sandy wrinkled her _____ when she frowned.

7. Keith drew a chair in the _____ of the picture.

Mythology

Mythology is a group of stories about the history of a people and their gods and heroes. Myths explain the beginnings of traditions, beliefs, or things and events in nature. The myths described below were told in ancient Greece to explain what causes thunder and lightning, the change of seasons, and falling in love. People still sometimes refer to these myths when discussing storms, the seasons, or love.

Thunder

The Greeks imagined Zeus riding in his chariot through the clouds. He was often pictured holding his thunderbolt. Zeus was lord of the sky, the rain-god, and the cloud-gatherer. When he became angry and threw his thunderbolt, people saw lightning and heard thunder.

The Change of Seasons

Hades was the god of the underworld. He married Persephone, the daughter of Demeter, who was goddess of agriculture. When her daughter went to live in the underworld, Demeter was so sad that she let the crops die. Then Zeus arranged for Persephone to live with her mother for six months of the year. While her daughter is with her, Demeter is happy. The earth blooms, and we have spring and summer. When Persephone leaves to return to Hades for the other six months of the year, Demeter is sad. Then the earth is brown, and we have fall and winter.

Two People Falling in Love

The Greeks believed that people fell in love when Eros, the god of love, shot an arrow into their hearts. Eros, sometimes called Cupid, is often shown as a winged boy on St. Valentine's Day cards. The picture of a heart and arrow is used to symbolize someone falling in love.

Sometimes Eros simply shot his arrows into the air. He often caused problems among people who were hit by his stray arrows. Other times Eros was kind, and he tried to reunite lovers with his arrows.

Think of another event or phenomenon, such as the fact that some birds fly south for the winter. Make up a myth that explains such an event. Use your own paper.

Classical Mythology

Classical mythology refers to the myths of the ancient Greeks and Romans. Much of what we know about classical Greek mythology comes from two long poems, the *Iliad* and the *Odyssey*, that are thought to be the work of the poet Homer, who lived in the 700s B.C. Many Roman gods and goddesses are similar to those of the Greeks due to contact between the two ancient cultures.

The ancient Greeks and Romans told stories to explain the birth of the gods and the beginning of the world. The Greeks believed that the first gods, the Titans, were the children of Gaea, or Earth, and Uranus, the ruler of the sky. Zeus, the son of the Titans Cronus and Rhea, became king of the gods when he defeated his father and the other Titans. He and the other gods and goddesses were believed to live on Mount Olympus.

Another word for god is *deity*. Here are some names of deities from classical Greek mythology.

➤ **Cronus**	son of Uranus and Gaea; the most powerful of the Titans; married his sister Rhea and fathered Zeus, Hades, Poseidon, Hera, Demeter, and Hestia; his Roman name was Saturn
➤ **Rhea**	sister and wife of Cronus; mother of Zeus; the Romans called her Ops
➤ **Oceanus**	a Titan who was the father of stream spirits and ocean nymphs
➤ **Hyperion**	a Titan who was the father of Helios (god of the sun), Aurora (goddess of the dawn), and Selene (goddess of the moon)
➤ **Phoebe**	a Titan who married her brother Coeus and became the grandmother of the goddess Artemis and the god Apollo; associated with the moon
➤ **Themis**	a Titan who was a goddess of wisdom, justice, and good counsel
➤ **Mnemosyne**	a Titan who was the goddess of memory and mother of the Muses
➤ **Muses**	nine sister goddesses of song, poetry, and the arts and sciences; daughters of Mnemosyne and Zeus
➤ **Iapetus**	a Titan who was the father of Atlas, Prometheus, and Epimetheus
➤ **Atlas**	a Titan whom Zeus punished by making him support the heavens on his shoulders
➤ **Prometheus**	a Titan who stole fire from the heavens and gave it to people
➤ **Epimetheus**	a Titan who married Pandora, the first woman

Answer each question below.

1. Who were the first gods in Greek mythology? _____

2. Which Titan held the earth on his shoulders? _____

3. What two poems tell us about Greek mythology? _____

4. Who was Gaea's husband? _____

5. Who gives inspiration to artists and poets? _____

The Olympians

Olympus is a mountain in Greece where the gods were supposed to live. The gods were the children and grandchildren of Cronus and Rhea, who were Titans. All of the gods on Olympus were called *Olympians.* The original Olympic Games were held in Greece to honor Zeus, the king of the gods.

Greek (Roman) Names of Some Olympians

➤ **Zeus (Jupiter)**   king of the gods; sender of thunder, lightning, rain, and winds

➤ **Hera (Juno)**   queen of the gods; goddess of women and marriage; sister and wife of Zeus

➤ **Poseidon (Neptune)** ruler of the sea and god of earthquakes; brother of Zeus; married to Amphitrite, granddaughter of the Titan Oceanus

➤ **Hades (Pluto)**   ruler of the underworld and the dead; brother of Zeus; also the god of wealth

➤ **Hestia (Vesta)**   goddess of the hearth and home; sister of Zeus

➤ **Demeter (Ceres)**   goddess of agriculture; sister of Zeus

Answer each question correctly.

1. How were Zeus and Poseidon related? _____

2. What was the Roman name for Hades, god of the underworld? _____

3. Name the queen of the gods, Zeus's wife. _____

4. What important sports event is named after Mount Olympus? _____

5. What did the Romans call Zeus? _____

6. Which Roman god might a seafood restaurant be named after? _____

7. What was the Roman name of the goddess of marriage? _____

8. When they heard thunder and saw lightning, the Greeks thought that one of the gods

   had thrown his thunderbolt. What was the name of this god? _____

9. Who were Demeter's sisters? _____

10. How many brothers did Demeter have? _____

Myths and Legends

There are many famous myths and legends from Greek and Roman mythology that are familiar stories in our culture. Here are a few examples.

Midas   You may have heard the expression "the Midas touch." Midas was a king who loved money very much. One of the gods, Dionysus, granted him one wish. Midas wished that everything he touched would turn into gold. The king was very happy until he found out that even his food turned into gold, and he almost starved to death. Midas begged Dionysus to take back his gift, which the god did.

Hercules   Hercules was the greatest hero of Greece and the strongest man on earth. His Greek name was Heracles, but he is often called by his Roman name, Hercules. You may have heard of the 12 labors of Hercules. These labors were 12 tasks that were thought to be impossible. Included in these tasks were the killing of a large lion and a hydra, a huge serpent with many heads. Hercules also had to clean the great stables of King Augeus in one day, which he did by turning rivers through them. His final labor was to capture Cerberus, the watchdog of the underworld. All of these tasks were impossible for anyone but Hercules to do. At the end of his life, Hercules was taken up to Mount Olympus and welcomed as one of the gods.

Pygmalion   In Greek mythology, Pygmalion was a king who fell in love with a statue of Aphrodite, the goddess of love and beauty. The Roman poet Ovid later retold this story. In Ovid's version, Pygmalion was a sculptor who made a beautiful ivory statue of a woman. Then he fell in love with his own creation. Aphrodite felt sorry for him and made the statue come to life as a real woman. Pygmalion later married this woman, Galatea. Versions of this legend have been retold by many writers. In the early 1900s, George Bernard Shaw based his play *Pygmalion* on the myth.

Echo   Have you ever heard an echo? One story tells how Hera became angry at a young girl named Echo, who liked to chatter. Hera forbade Echo ever to speak again, except to repeat what someone else said to her. A different legend tells how Echo loved Narcissus, who did not love her back. Echo pined away until only her voice remained.

Answer each question below.

1. Which story illustrates that greed does not pay? _____

2. The musical comedy *My Fair Lady* is about an Englishman who taught a poor, young flower girl how to speak and act like a duchess, and then fell in love with her. Which myth is this story based on?

_____

3. Describe three of the 12 labors of Hercules. _____

_____

Norse Mythology

The Vikings, or Norsemen, of Scandinavia reached North America in about A.D.1000, almost 500 years before the arrival of Christopher Columbus. The gods and goddesses of Norse mythology are also important in our language. Here are some names from Norse mythology.

- ➤ **Asgard**   the home of the Norse gods
- ➤ **Odin**   ruler of the gods; god of war and poets; the magician god; protector of heroes; also called *Woden*
- ➤ **Frigg**   goddess of marriage; wife of Odin and mother of Balder
- ➤ **Balder**   the favorite of the gods; son of Odin and Frigg; died after being struck by a piece of mistletoe, the only thing that could harm him
- ➤ **Thor**   the god of thunder and lightning; protected the gods and goddesses from their enemies, the giants; carried a hammer
- ➤ **Freyr**   god of peace, rain, and sunshine; son of the sea god Njörd and brother of Freyja
- ➤ **Freyja**   goddess of love, battle, and death; sister of Freyr
- ➤ **Heimdall**   watchman of the gods; guarded the rainbow bridge to Asgard
- ➤ **Tyr**   god of justice and the rules of war; one of the earliest Norse gods
- ➤ **Hel**   goddess of death (Hel was also the name of the underworld)

A The following chart shows Norse, Roman, and Greek deities. Write the names of the missing gods and goddesses on the lines provided below. If necessary, refer back to the earlier pages in this unit.

	Norse	Greek	Roman
1. god of war	_____	Ares	_____
2. goddess of love	Freyja	_____	Venus
3. deity of agriculture	Freyr	Demeter	_____
4. deity of the underworld	_____	_____	Pluto
5. king of the gods	_____	Zeus	_____

B Answer the following questions.

1. Who is goddess of the dead in Norse mythology? _____

2. Ares is the Greek god of war. Who is the Norse god of war? _____

3. Name the chief god in Norse mythology. _____

4. Who was Odin's wife? _____

5. The Greek gods lived in Olympia. The Norse gods lived in _____

6. Who guarded the rainbow bridge that led into Asgard? _____

7. Who was the Norse goddess of love? _____

8. Who was the Norse god of thunder? _____

9. What is the relationship between Odin and Balder? _____

Names of the Planets

The word *planet* comes from the Greek word *planasthai,* which means "to wander." All of the planets in our solar system are named after Roman and Greek gods.

The Solar System

Mercury is the planet closest to the sun and travels around the sun the fastest. It was named after the swift messenger of the ancient Roman gods.

Venus is often called the *morning star* because it can sometimes be seen at sunrise. It is the second planet from the sun. Venus was named after the Roman goddess of love and beauty.

Earth is the third planet from the sun and the only planet in our solar system to support life. *Earth* is another name for Gaea, the Greek deity who was a symbol of the planet and who was known as the giver of dreams and the caretaker of plants and children.

Mars was named after the Roman god of war because its reddish color resembles blood.

Jupiter is the largest planet. It was named after the king of the Roman gods and the ruler of all people on earth. Jupiter was the son of Saturn, the father of Mars and Venus, and a brother to Pluto and Neptune.

Saturn is the second largest planet and is known for the seven large rings that encircle it. It was named after the son of Uranus, the ruler of the heavens in Greek and Roman mythology. Saturn conquered Uranus to become lord of the universe.

Uranus was the ruler of the heavens in Greek mythology. He was the husband of Gaea (Earth) and also the father of the Titans. He was overthrown by his son Cronus, also called Saturn.

Neptune is the eighth planet from the sun. It was named after the Roman god of the sea.

Pluto is the darkest planet and farthest away from the sun. It was named after the Roman god of the underworld.

Explain the reasons for the name of each planet.

1. Pluto _____

2. Jupiter _____

3. Venus _____

4. Mercury _____

5. Mars _____

Calendar Words

Mythology also surrounds us in everyday life because of its use in our calendar words.

Days of the Week	
Monday	the moon's day
Tuesday	Tyr's day
Wednesday	Woden's (Odin's) day
Thursday	Thor's day
Friday	Frigg's day
Saturday	Saturn's day
Sunday	the sun's day

Thor

A Who was each day of the week named after? If the day was named after a god or goddess, identify the deity and the mythology.

Example: Venus, Roman goddess of love and beauty

1. Monday _____

2. Tuesday _____

3. Wednesday _____

4. Thursday _____

5. Friday _____

6. Saturday _____

7. Sunday _____

B Identify the day named for each Norse deity described below. Then write the names of the Greek and Roman deities who were similar to the Norse ones.

	Day	Greek deity	Roman deity
1. Norse god of thunder	_____	_____	_____
2. queen of Norse gods	_____	_____	_____
3. Norse god of war	_____	_____	_____
4. king of Norse gods	_____	_____	_____

Months of the Year

The names of the months have come down to us from the ancient Romans. The early Roman calendar was made up of only 10 months; January and February were added in about 700 B.C.

➤ **January**   the Roman month of Januarius; named after Janus, the god of doorways and beginnings

➤ **February**   the Roman month of Februarius; named after Februus, the Roman festival of purification

➤ **March**   the Roman month of Martius; named after Mars, the god of war

➤ **April**   the Roman month of Aprilis; may have been named after Aphrodite, the Greek goddess of love and beauty, or the name may have been taken from the Latin word *aperire*, meaning "to open," in reference to the opening of buds in the spring

➤ **May**   the Roman month of Maius; named after the goddess Maia

➤ **June**   the Roman month of Junius; probably named after Juno, queen of the gods

➤ **July**   the Roman month of Julius; named after Julius Caesar, who ruled Rome from 49 to 44 B.C.

➤ **August**   the Roman month of Augustus; named after Augustus Caesar, who ruled Rome from 43 B.C. to A.D. 14.

➤ **September**   seventh month of the early Roman calendar (*septem* means "seven")

➤ **October**   eighth month of the early Roman calendar (*octo* means "eight")

➤ **November**   ninth month of the early Roman calendar (*novem* means "nine")

➤ **December**   tenth month of the early Roman calendar (*decem* means "ten")

A Who was each month named after? If the month was named after a god or goddess, identify the mythology (Greek, Roman, Norse).

1. January_____

2. March_____

3. May_____

4. June_____

5. July_____

6. August_____

B Write the meanings of these Latin root words.

1. novem   _____   4. aperire   _____

2. octo   _____   5. septem   _____

3. decem   _____

Vocabulary Builder

Many descriptive words and phrases have come from Greek myths and legends.

➤ **Achilles' heel**   a vulnerable spot; a weakness. When Achilles was born, his mother dipped him in the river Styx to protect him from harm. She was careless and did not see that the water did not cover his heel. Achilles grew to become one of the greatest of all Greek warriors. At the battle of Troy, Paris shot an arrow which struck Achilles in his heel and killed him.

➤ **ambrosia**   the food of the gods; anything that tastes very delicious

➤ **nymph**   Greek or Roman nature goddess who lived in rivers, mountains, or trees. Echo was a nymph.

➤ **odyssey**   a long journey; from the long trip of the warrior Odysseus on his return from the Trojan War; it was described by the Greek poet Homer in his story, the *Odyssey.* In Latin, Odysseus was called *Ulysses.*

➤ **Pandora's box**   a source of troubles. In Greek mythology, Pandora was the first woman. She received a box which she was not supposed to open. She became curious and opened the box. Inside were all of the troubles of the world (poverty, illness, war, etc.), which then escaped. Today, "opening Pandora's box" means allowing a series of bad events to begin.

➤ **satyr**   from Greek mythology, a woodland god; often pictured as a man with a goat's legs, ears, and horns

➤ **Troy**   an ancient city in Asia Minor (now Turkey) described in Greek and Roman legends as the site of a great battle between the Trojans and Greeks

Fill in the blanks with the word or phrase that completes each sentence.

1. Ambrosia is "food for the _____."

2. Everyone says that John's pride is his _____.

3. Ivan thought that lowering fines for overdue books would open a

   _____ of problems for the library.

4. A _____ was a creature that was half-man and half-goat.

5. Achilles was a Greek warrior who died in the battle of _____.

6. Achilles' mother was a _____, one of the Greek goddesses that lived in the rivers, mountains, or trees.

7. Zeus, Hera, and Demeter are all Greek _____.

8. Achilles' mother dipped him in the river called _____.

9. _____ killed Achilles at the battle of Troy.

10. In the classical Greek story, the _____, Homer tells of Odysseus' long trip home from Troy.

Review Units 11–13

A Answer each of these questions on your own paper.

1. What is the difference between a hurricane and a typhoon?

2. In what part of the world do trade winds occur?

3. What does a weather vane tell about the weather?

4. From which direction does a zephyr blow?

5. What are three special types of cyclones?

B Fill in the blank with the term that best completes each sentence.

1. The children of your parents' first cousins are your _____.
   a. cousins-in-law   b. second cousins   c. third cousins

2. The wife of your brother is your _____.
   a. sister-in-law   b. cousin   c. stepsister

3. Stepparents and their stepchildren are _____.
   a. related by blood   b. not related   c. related by marriage

4. All of your ancestors together make up your _____.
   a. progeny   b. ancestry   c. heirs

5. Another word for ancestors is _____.
   a. grandparents   b. forerunners   c. forebears

C Complete the paragraphs below.

The mythologies of Greece, Rome, and Scandinavia show interesting similarities. In Greek mythology, the gods and goddesses lived on 1._____; the Norse deities also lived in a special place, called 2._____. The gods and goddesses were ruled by a king and queen who were called 3._____ and 4._____ by the Greeks, 5._____ and 6._____ by the Romans, and 7._____ and 8._____ by the Scandinavians.

The planets were named after Greek and Roman gods and goddesses. 9._____ was named after the Roman goddess of love and beauty, and Pluto, the farthest planet from the sun, was named after the Roman god of 10._____.

Several of the days of the week were named after Norse deities. For example, Thursday was named after the Norse god of thunder and lightning, 11._____. Friday was named after 12._____, the goddess of marriage. 13._____ was named after Tyr, the god of justice.

End-of-Book Test

A Read the sentences below. Use your knowledge of prefixes, suffixes, and root words to figure out what each underlined word means.

1. The library saved space by storing old magazines on underline{microfilm}.
   a. film with very small images
   b. film with very large images
   c. film with few images

2. George went to the dentist for his underline{semiannual} checkup.
   a. yearly
   b. twice a year
   c. monthly

3. The doctor was a very underline{credible} witness during the trial.
   a. unreliable
   b. fair
   c. believable

4. The underline{powerless} citizens could do nothing about the oncoming tornado.
   a. without power
   b. full of power
   c. having limited power

5. After the war, the prisoners were underline{liberated}.
   a. interviewed
   b. treated kindly
   c. set free

6. The eagle underline{expanded} its wings as it flew away from the nest.
   a. brought forward
   b. tucked under
   c. spread out

7. Japan is one of the most underline{populous} countries in the world.
   a. polluted
   b. containing many people
   c. remote

8. Ilene underline{predetermined} how much she would spend for a new car.
   a. decided before
   b. thought about after
   c. adjusted again

9. There are many underline{bilingual} signs in Quebec, Canada.
   a. written in many languages
   b. written in two languages
   c. written in one language

10. The underline{botanist} developed a rose that was resistant to disease.
    a. the study of plants
    b. a person who is afraid of plants
    c. a person who studies plants

11. Mr. Martinez underline{terminated} his contract with the freight company.
    a. extended
    b. ended
    c. financed

12. Shelley underline{postponed} her trip to Australia until July.
    a. delayed
    b. rescheduled
    c. arranged

13. Dr. Clark is a highly respected underline{cardiologist}.
    a. children's doctor
    b. heart doctor
    c. eye doctor

14. The author underline{autographed} copies of her new bestseller.
    a. signed by someone else
    b. signed herself
    c. edited by someone else

15. The photographer used a underline{telephoto} lens on her camera.
    a. makes faraway images larger
    b. makes nearby images larger
    c. makes images more colorful

16. Our family underline{recycles} aluminum cans and bottles.
    a. divides
    b. uses before
    c. processes again

B Match the words with their definitions.

____	1. century	a.	someone seeking a job
____	2. transcript	b.	person you are married to
____	3. premium	c.	money taken out of your gross pay
____	4. precipitation	d.	official educational history
____	5. debt	e.	group of several related families
____	6. spouse	f.	money that is owed
____	7. gross pay	g.	moisture in the form of rain, sleet, snow, or hail
____	8. jargon	h.	person who rents a piece of property
____	9. clan	i.	store where you can buy medicines
____	10. pharmacy	j.	total amount of money earned
____	11. applicant	k.	average weather conditions over a period of time
____	12. deductions	l.	technical language
____	13. tenant	m.	100 years
____	14. climate	n.	fee for insurance

C Complete each sentence with one of the words.

true-blue	high-rise	weatherproof	self-service	forecast
time-out	good-natured	brainstormed	artificial	descendant

1. We don't have to worry about camping in the rain because our tent is _____ .

2. Mike pumped his own gas at the _____ station.

3. The team had only one _____ left in the game.

4. A _____ friend sticks by you through good and bad times.

5. Lin is so _____ that it is a pleasure to work with her.

6. We took the elevator to the twenty-fifth floor of the _____ .

7. Those _____ flowers almost look real!

8. Larry _____ about how to raise money for new band uniforms.

9. The 30-day _____ predicted warmer than usual weather.

10. Tom is a _____ of a famous inventor.